Wireless Java™:
Developing with Java 2,
Micro Edition

JONATHAN KNUDSEN

Wireless Java™: Developing with Jave 2, Micro Edition
Copyright ©2001 by Jonathan Knudsen

ISBN (pbk): 1-893115-50-X
Printed and bound in the United States of America 12345678910

Trademarked names may appear in this book. Rather than use a trademark symbol with every occurrence of a trademarked name, we use the names only in an editorial fashion and to the benefit of the trademark owner, with no intention of infringement of the trademark.

Editorial Directors: Dan Appleman, Gary Cornell, Karen Watterson
Assistant Editorial Director: Jason Gilmore
Managing Editor: Grace Wong
Technical Reviewer: Nicolas Lorain
Editor: Kari Brooks
Page Composition: Diana Van Winkle, Van Winkle Design Group
Artist: Tony Jonick, Rappid Rabbit Publishing
Indexer: Valerie Perry
Cover Design: Karl Miyajima

Distributed to the book trade in the United States by Springer-Verlag New York, Inc., 175 Fifth Avenue, New York, NY, 10010 and outside the United States by Springer-Verlag GmbH & Co. KG, Tiergartenstr. 17, 69112 Heidelberg, Germany

In the United States, phone 1-800-SPRINGER;
orders@springer-ny.com; http://www.springer-ny.com
Outside the United States, contact orders@springer.de; http://www.springer.de;
fax +49 6221 345229

For information on translations, please contact Apress directly at
901 Grayson Street, Suite 204, Berkeley, CA, 94710
Phone: 510-549-5937; Fax: 510-549-5939; info@apress.com;
http://www.apress.com

The information in this book is distributed on an "as is" basis, without warranty. Although every precaution has been taken in the preparation of this work, neither the author nor Apress shall have any liability to any person or entity with respect to any loss or damage caused or alleged to be caused directly or indirectly by the information contained in this work.

To Andrew and Elena

Contents at a Glance

v

Contents

Preface

This book describes how to program mobile telephones, pagers, and other small devices using Java™ technology. It is about the Mobile Information Device Profile (MIDP), which is part of Java 2 Platform, Micro Edition (J2ME™). It is concise and complete, describing all of MIDP, as well as moving into several advanced topics like XML and cryptography.

Who Are You?

You're probably reading this book because you're excited about building wireless applications with Java. This book is aimed at people who already have experience programming in Java. At a minimum, you should understand the Java programming language and the fundamentals of object oriented programming. Some chapters delve into subjects that themselves could occupy entire books. These chapters include suggested reading if you want to come up to speed on a particular subject.

If you are unfamiliar with Java, I suggest you read an introductory book or take a course. *Learning Java* (O'Reilly 2000) is a good introduction to Java for programmers who are already experienced in another language such as C or C++.

The Structure of This Book

This book is organized into twelve chapters and one appendix. There are basically three sections. The first two chapters are introductory material. Chapters 3 through 9 provide complete coverage of the MIDP APIs. Chapters 10 through 12 cover advanced topics. The complete breakdown of chapters is listed here:

- Chapter 1, "Introduction," provides context and motivation for the rest of the book. J2ME is explained in detail, gradually zooming in to MIDP.

- Chapter 2, "Building MIDlets," is intended to be a teaser. It includes an example application that allows you to look up the definitions of words over the Internet using any MIDP device. Along the way you'll learn a lot about developing applications for the MIDP platform.

- Chapter 3, "All About MIDlets," goes into detail about the life cycle and packaging of MIDP applications.

- Chapter 4, "Almost the Same Old Stuff," describes the pieces of the MIDP API that will be familiar to Java programmers.

- Chapter 5, "Creating a User Interface," is the first of three chapters devoted to MIDP's user-interface packages. It provides an overview of MIDP's user-interface package and goes into detail about the simple visual components.

- Chapter 6, "Lists and Forms," picks up where Chapter 5 left off, describing MIDP's advanced user-interface components.

- Chapter 7, "Persistent Storage," describes MIDP's mechanism for storing data.

- Chapter 8, "Connecting to the World," contains all the juicy details about how MIDP applications can send and receive data over the Internet.

- Chapter 9, "Programming a Game Interface," is the third chapter about user interface. It describes the low level, or "game," API that can be used for specialized application user interfaces.

- Chapter 10, "Performance," describes techniques for coping with the limited resources that are available on small devices.

- Chapter 11, "Parsing XML," examines the spectrum of small XML parsers that are currently available. It describes how to port parsers to MIDP and briefly discusses the usage involves with each parser.

- Chapter 12, "Protecting Network Data," discusses how to protect valuable data on the insecure Internet. It includes two sample applications that demonstrate cryptographic techniques for protecting data.

- Finally, an Appendix contains a complete API reference for the classes and interfaces that make up MIDP. The method signatures for the public API of each class and interface are listed for handy quick reference.

Acknowledgments

It's been said that it takes a village to raise a child—it's kind of the same thing with a book. Thanks to all the wonderful folks at Apress for helping me bring this book to the world. First, thanks to Gary Cornell for believing in me enough to sign this book. Grace Wong was the project manager; she deserves a big shiny medal for her patient revisions to the book's schedule. Kari Brooks, my copyeditor, helped me polish my writing to its current, fine sheen. Nicolas Lorain was kind enough to step in as our emergency technical editor—thanks for keeping me honest about the technical details.

Most of all, I would like to thank my family, who put up with me while I proved I had the machismo to write a book *outside* of my day job. Kristen, thanks for being so beautiful, inside and out. You are most amazing person I know. Our children—Daphne, Luke, Andrew, and Elena—will probably thinks it's very funny some day that mobile telephones used to come with just a few megs of memory and have piddly network speeds like 9.6 Kbps. Maybe they'll be the ones to push computing out of its stone age. Whatever they do, I will love them. I'm a very lucky man.

CHAPTER 1

Introduction

Java™ 2 Platform, Micro Edition (J2ME™) is the second revolution in Java's short history. When Java was introduced in 1995, it looked like the future of computing was in *applets*, small programs that could be downloaded and run on demand. A slow Internet forced applets out of the mainstream. Java, as a platform, did not really take off until the advent of *servlets*, Java programs that run on a server (essentially a replacement for CGI). Java further expanded into the server side of things, eventually picking up the moniker of Java 2 Platform, Enterprise Edition (J2EE™). This was the first revolution, the blitz of server-side Java.

The second revolution is the explosion of small-device Java, and it's happening now. The market for small devices is expanding rapidly, and Java is important for two reasons. First, developers can write code and have it run on dozens of small platforms, without change. Second, Java has some important safety features for downloadable code.

Understanding J2ME

J2ME isn't really a specific piece of software or specification. All it means is Java for small devices. Small devices range in size from pagers, mobile phones, personal digital assistants (PDAs), all the way up to things like set-top boxes that are just shy of being desktop PCs.

J2ME is divided into *configurations* and *profiles*, which provide specific information about APIs and different families of devices. A configuration is designed for a specific kind of device based on memory constraints and processor power. It usually specifies a Java Virtual Machine (JVM) that can be easily ported to devices supporting the configuration. It also specifies some subset of the Java 2 Platform, Standard Edition (J2SE™) APIs that will be used on the platform, as well as additional APIs that may be necessary.

Profiles are more specific than configurations. A profile is based on a configuration and adds APIs for user interface, persistent storage, and whatever else is necessary to develop running applications.

Currently, there is a handful of configurations and profiles under development, as illustrated in Figure 1-1.

1

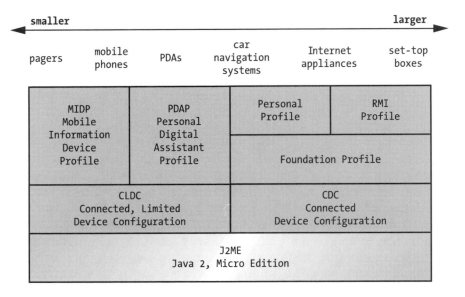

Figure 1-1. The J2ME universe

Configurations

A configuration specifies a JVM and some set of core APIs for a specific family of devices. Currently there are two.

Connected Device Configuration (CDC)

A connected device has, at a minimum, 512KB of read-only memory (ROM), 256KB of random access memory (RAM), and some kind of network connection. The CDC is designed for devices like television set-top boxes, car navigation systems, and high end PDAs. The CDC specifies that a full Java Virtual Machine (as defined in the Java Virtual Machine Specification, 2nd edition) must be supported.

The configurations and profiles of J2ME are generally described in terms of their memory capacity. Usually a minimum amount of ROM and RAM is specified. For small devices, it makes sense to think in terms of volatile and non-volatile memory. The *non-volatile memory* is capable of keeping its contents intact as the device is turned on and off. ROM is one type of non-volatile memory, but this could also be flash memory or memory-backed RAM. *Volatile memory* is essentially workspace and does not maintain its contents when the device is turned off.

The CDC is being developed under the Java Community Process[SM]. For more information on the CDC, see http://java.sun.com/products/cdc/. A Linux reference implementation is available.

The Java Community Process^{SM}

J2ME configurations and profiles are created under the aegis of the Java Community Process (JCP). The JCP is designed to insure that Java technology is developed according to community consensus. The process is described here: `http://java.sun.com/aboutJava/communityprocess/`.

Configurations and profiles first appear in the world as Java Specification Requests (JSRs). You can see a list of current JSRs here: `http://java.sun.com/aboutJava/communityprocess/search.html`.

Connected, Limited Device Configuration (CLDC)

CLDC is the configuration that interests us, because it encompasses mobile phones, pagers, PDAs, and other devices of similar size. CLDC is aimed at smaller devices than the CDC. The name is a little misleading; really, the CLDC is designed for a small device with a limited network connection—"Limited Connection Device Configuration" might have been more accurate.

The CLDC is designed for devices with 160KB to 512KB of memory available for the Java platform. If you've ever watched J2SE gobble up tens of megabytes of memory on your desktop computer, you'll appreciate the challenge of J2ME. The "limited connection" simply refers to a network connection that is intermittent and probably not very fast. (Most mobile telephones, for example, typically achieve data rates of 9.6Kbps.) Between the small screen size, limited memory, and slow network connection, applications designed in the CLDC space should be very sparing with the use of the network connection.

The CLDC is based around a small JVM called the KVM. Its name comes from the fact that it is a JVM whose size is measured in kilobytes rather than megabytes. While the CLDC is a specifications document, the KVM refers to a specific piece of software.[1] Because of its small size, the KVM can't do everything a JVM does in the J2SE world.

- Native methods cannot be added at runtime. All native functionality is built into the KVM.

- The KVM only includes a subset of the standard bytecode verifier. This means that the task of verifying classes is split between the CLDC device and some external mechanism. This has serious security implications, as we'll discuss later.

---

1. The KVM was originally part of Spotless, a Sun research project. See `http://www.sun.com/research/spotless/`.

You can find more information at the CLDC home page, `http://java.sun.com/products/cldc/`. For a full list of differences between KVM and JVM, see the technical article on `http://developer.java.sun.com/developer/technicalArticles/wireless/midpapi/`.

Building Blocks

In the next generation of J2ME, a concept called Building Blocks will replace configurations. A *Building Block* is just some subset of a J2SE API. For example, one Building Block might be created from a subset of the J2SE `java.io` package. Conceptually, it represents a smaller chunk of information than a configuration. Profiles, then, will be built on top of a set of Building Blocks rather than a configuration.

The definition of Building Blocks is itself a JSR, which is briefly described here: `http://java.sun.com/aboutJava/communityprocess/jsr/jsr_068_j2me.html`.

Profiles

A profile is layered on top of a configuration (and someday, on Building Blocks), adding the APIs and specifications necessary to develop applications for a specific family of devices.

Profiles in Progress

Several different profiles are being developed under the Java Community Process. Table 1-1 provides a birds-eye view.

Table 1-1. J2ME Profiles

NAME	JSR	ROM	RAM	BASE
Foundation	46	1024KB	512KB	CDC
Personal	62	2.5MB	1MB	CDC + Foundation Profile
RMI	66	2.5MB	1MB	CDC + Foundation Profile
MIDP	37	128KB	32KB	CLDC
PDA	75	~256 KB	~256KB	CLDC

The Foundation Profile is a fundamental specification for devices that can support a rich-networked J2ME environment. It does not support a user interface; other profiles can be layered on top of the Foundation Profile to add user interface support and other functionality.

Layered on top of the Foundation Profile are the Personal Profile and the RMI Profile. The combination of CDC + Foundation Profile + Personal Profile is designed as the next generation of the PersonalJava™ application runtime environment (see `http://java.sun.com/products/personaljava/`). As such, the Personal Profile has the specific goal of backward compatibility with previous versions of Personal Java.

The RMI Profile is also built on top of the Foundation Profile. As the name implies, this profile is designed for smallish devices that will support RMI, and by extension, JINI. (RMI is Remote Method Invocation, Java's distributed object technology. JINI is a technology for dynamic, pluggable networked devices. For more information, see `http://java.sun.com/products/jini/`.) This is a larger scale than we'll be talking about; space is at such a premium in devices like mobile phones that there's simply not room for the Reflection API, RMI, or JINI.

The PDA Profile is designed for palmtop devices with a minimum of 512KB combined ROM and RAM (and a maximum of 16MB). It will probably use a subset of the J2SE Abstract Windowing Toolkit (AWT) for graphic user interface.

Mobile Information Device Profile (MIDP)

The focus of this book is the Mobile Information Device Profile (MIDP). According to the specification, a Mobile Information Device (MID) has the following characteristics:

- 128KB of non-volatile memory for the MIDP implementation

- 32KB of volatile memory for the runtime heap

- 8KB of non-volatile memory for persistent data

- A screen of at least 96×54 pixels

- Some capacity for input, either by keypad, keyboard, or touch screen

- Two-way network connection, possibly intermittent

Try to imagine a device that might be a MID: mobile telephones and advanced pagers are right in the groove, but entry-level PDAs could also fit this description.

More information about MIDP, including a link to the official specification document, is at `http://java.sun.com/products/midp/`.

Or you could just keep reading.

Anatomy of MIDP Applications

The APIs available to a MIDP application come from packages in both the CLDC and the MIDP, as shown in Figure 1-2.

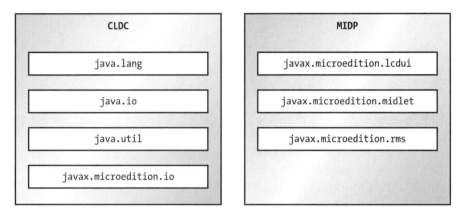

Figure 1-2. MIDP packages

The CLDC defines a core of APIs, mostly taken from the J2SE world. These include fundamental language classes in java.lang, stream classes from java.io, and simple collections from java.util. The CLDC also specifies a generalized network API in javax.microedition.io.

Optionally, device vendors may also supply Java APIs to access device-specific features. MIDs, then, will typically be able to run several different flavors of applications. Figure 1-3 shows a map of the possibilities.

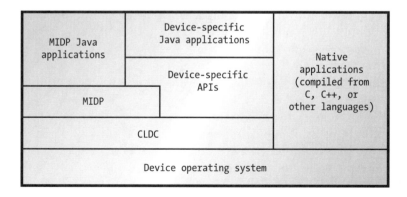

Figure 1-3. MID software components

Each device implements some kind of operating system (OS). Native applications run directly on this layer and represent the world as it is today—many different kinds of devices, each with its own OS and native applications.

Layered on top of the device OS is the CLDC (including the KVM) and the MIDP APIs. MIDP applications use only the CLDC and MIDP APIs. Device-specific Java applications may also use Java APIs supplied by the device vendor.

Advantages of MIDP

Given the spectrum of configurations and profiles, why is this book about MIDP? First, MIDP comes at a critical time, a time when MIDs like mobile phones are an exploding market. Simultaneously, MIDs are achieving the kind of processing power, memory consumption, and Internet connectivity that makes them an attractive platform for distributed applications.

Second, of course, MIDP is the first J2ME profile that is ready for prime time. If you read into the next chapter, you can write MIDP applications today.

Portability

The advantage of using Java over using other tools for MID application development is portability. You could write MID applications with C or C++, but the result would be specific to a single platform. An application written using the MIDP APIs will be directly portable to any MIDP device.

If you've been following Java's development for any time, this should sound familiar. It's the same "Write Once, Run Anywhere™" (WORA) mantra that Sun's been repeating since 1995. Unfortunately, WORA is a bit of a four-letter word for developers who struggled with cross-platform issues in JDK 1.0 and JDK 1.1 (particularly the browser implementations). While Java's cross-platform capabilities in Java 2 are generally successful, WORA still has a taint of unfulfilled promise.

Should you wait for MIDP 2 before you try to write cross-platform applications for small devices? I think not. I believe MIDP 1.0 can work as advertised because the scale is so much smaller than it is with desktop Java. Less code means fewer bugs when porting to multiple platforms. Most of the cross-platform incompatibilities of JDK 1.0 and JDK 1.1 were caused by the nightmare of trying to fit disparate windowing systems into the AWT's peer-based component architecture. MIDP has nothing approaching the complexity of AWT, which means there's an excellent possibility that MIDP applications will seamlessly run on multiple platforms right out of the starting gate. Furthermore, while the JDK 1.0 test suite only included a few dozen tests, the MIDP compatibility test suite includes several thousand tests.

Security

A second, slightly less compelling reason for using Java for MID development is security. Java is well known for its ability to safely run downloaded code like applets. This seems like a perfect fit—it's easy to imagine nifty applications dynamically downloading to your mobile phone.

But it's not quite such a rosy picture. For one thing, the KVM used in the CLDC only implements a partial bytecode verifier, which means that part of the important task of bytecode verification is performed off the MID.

Second, the CLDC does not allow for application-defined classloaders. This means that any kind of dynamic application delivery is dependent on device-specific mechanisms. As you'll see, application deployment is not specifically defined in the CLDC or MIDP.

MIDP applications do offer one important security promise: they can never escape from the confines of the KVM. This means that, barring bugs, a MIDP application will never be able to write to device memory that doesn't belong to the KVM. A MIDP application will never mess up another application on the same device or the device OS itself.[2]

MIDP Vendors

Several large players have thrown their weight behind the MIDP. A quick browse of the JSR page for MIDP exposes the most important companies.

Two Asian companies led the charge to provide network services for Java-enabled mobile phones. In Korea, LG TeleCom deployed a service called ez-i™ in mid-2000. Later that same year, NTT DoCoMo deployed their wildy popular i-mode™. The APIs developed for LG TeleCom and NTT DoCoMo were similar to MIDP but were completed before the MIDP specification.

In the United States, Motorola was the first manufacturer to produce a MIDP telephone. The i50sx and i85s were released on April 2, 2001, with service provided by Nextel.

The expert group that created the MIDP specification includes an impressive list of manufacturers—Ericsson, Hitachi, Nokia, Sony, Symbian. Over the next twelve months, you'll probably see more MIDP devices arriving on the market.

---

2. A MIDP application could conceivably launch a denial-of-service attack, (i.e., sucking up all the processor's time or bringing the device OS to a standstill). It's widely acknowledged that there's not much defense against denial-of-service attacks. Applications and applets in J2SE suffer from the same vulnerability.

The Future of MIDP

What's ahead for MIDP? This book covers the MIDP 1.0 specification, but of course the ink is hardly dry on the paper before MIDP 1.1 will come along. As of this writing, a new JSR has been created for the next generation of MIDP. Some information about the JSR is available at `http://java.sun.com/aboutJava/communityprocess/jsr/jsr_118_midpng.html`.

According to that page, the next generation MIDP specification will address several new areas, including the following:

- Security and HTTPS support

- Socket and datagram network connectivity

- XML parsing

By reading this book, you're already ahead of the curve—you'll learn about parsing XML in Chapter 11 and cryptography in Chapter 12.

According to the Web page, the new specification will be developed in Q1–Q2, 2002.

Summary

J2ME is the Java platform for small devices, a broad field that covers pretty much everything smaller than a breadbox. Because J2ME spans such a diverse selection of hardware, it is divided into configurations and profiles. A configuration specifies a subset of J2SE functionality and the behavior of the JVM, while profiles are generally more specific to a family of devices with similar characteristics. The Mobile Information Device Profile, which is the focus of this book, discusses APIs for devices like mobile phones and two-way pagers.

CHAPTER 2

Building MIDlets

MIDP applications are piquantly called MIDlets, a continuation of the naming theme begun by *applets* and *servlets*. Writing MIDlets is relatively easy for a moderately experienced Java programmer. After all, the programming language is still Java. Furthermore, many of the fundamental APIs from java.lang and java.io are basically the same in the MIDP as they are in J2SE. Learning the new APIs (in the javax.microedition hierarchy) is not terribly difficult, as you'll see in the remainder of this book.

The actual development process, however, is a little more complicated for MIDlets than it is for J2SE applications. Beyond a basic compile-and-run cycle, MIDlets require some additional tweaking and a deployment step, either to an actual device or to a device emulator. To show how things work, and to give you a taste of MIDlet development, this chapter is dedicated to building and running a simple MIDlet. In later chapters, we'll delve into the details of the MIDP APIs. In this chapter, you'll get a feel for the big picture of MIDlet development.

Getting Started

MIDlets are developed on regular desktop computers, although the MIDlet itself is designed to run on a small device. To develop MIDlets, you'll need some kind of development kit, either from Sun or another vendor. Remember, the MIDP is only a specification; vendors are free to develop their own implementations.

Sun offers two flavors of MIDP. The first is the MIDP reference implementation, which contains API documentation, build tools, and an emulator (Windows only) for a mobile phone. It is available here:

```
http://javashoplm.sun.com/ECom/docs/Welcome.jhtml?
    StoreId=5&PartDetailId=MIDP-1.0-WIN-G-CS&TransactionId=communitySource
```

The URL is split across two lines for readability. You will need to register to download the MIDP reference implementation, but there is no charge for registration.

Sun also offers the J2ME Wireless Toolkit, a collection of software built around the MIDP reference implementation. The Wireless Toolkit (or J2MEWTK, as it's awkwardly known) includes the reference implementation and a GUI tool that greatly simplifies the process of building and packaging applications. The J2MEWTK is available here: `http://java.sun.com/products/j2mewtoolkit/`.

Motorola also has a MIDP development kit, although you'll have to register (at no cost) to download it. You can find this kit at `http://www.idendev.com/`.

Research In Motion distributes a MIDP development kit to support their Blackberry product line of mobile e-mail devices. You can find it here: `http://developers.rim.net/handhelds/software/jde/java.shtml`.

Finally, Zucotto Wireless makes a MIDP development kit to support their hardware products. You can download the development kit at `http://www.zucotto.com/whiteboard/`.

Download and install whatever development kit you wish. I'll be using the J2MEWTK throughout the rest of the book. You'll notice this most in this chapter, where I'll go into detail about the build tools and the emulators. For much of the remainder of this book, I'll simply be walking through the MIDP APIs, so it won't really matter which development kit you're running.

Creating Source Code

Writing Java source code is the same as it always was: use your favorite text editor to create a source file with a .java extension. The example we'll build and run is Jargoneer, a MIDlet that looks up words in the Jargon File. The Jargon File is a comprehensive lexicon of hacker slang (find out more by visiting `http://www.fwi.uva.nl/~mes/jargon/`).

Jargoneer allows you to enter any word, and then connects to an Internet site to find the definition. Running this MIDlet will allow you to appear cool in the company of your hacker friends. When someone uses an unfamiliar word, like "cruft" or "grok," you can surreptitiously key the word into your mobile phone and see a definition in a few seconds.

Jargoneer's source code is provided in Listing 2-1. If you don't want to type it in, you can download all of the code examples in this book from `http://www.apress.com`.

Listing 2-1. Jargoneer's source code.

```java
import java.io.*;

import javax.microedition.io.*;
import javax.microedition.midlet.*;
import javax.microedition.lcdui.*;

public class Jargoneer extends MIDlet
    implements CommandListener {
  private Display mDisplay;

  private Command mExitCommand, mFindCommand, mCancelCommand;

  private TextBox mSubmitBox;
  private Form mProgressForm;
  private StringItem mProgressString;
  private Gauge mProgressGauge;

  public Jargoneer() {
    mExitCommand = new Command("Exit", Command.EXIT, 0);
    mFindCommand = new Command("Find", Command.SCREEN, 0);
    mCancelCommand = new Command("Cancel", Command.CANCEL, 0);

    mSubmitBox = new TextBox("Jargoneer", "", 32, 0);
    mSubmitBox.addCommand(mExitCommand);
    mSubmitBox.addCommand(mFindCommand);
    mSubmitBox.setCommandListener(this);

    mProgressForm = new Form("Lookup progress");
    mProgressGauge = new Gauge(null, false, 10, 0);
    mProgressString = new StringItem(null, null);
    mProgressForm.append(mProgressGauge);
    mProgressForm.append(mProgressString);
  }

  public void startApp() {
    mDisplay = Display.getDisplay(this);

    mDisplay.setCurrent(mSubmitBox);
  }

public void pauseApp() {}
  public void destroyApp(boolean unconditional) {}
```

```
            public void commandAction(Command c, Displayable s) {
              if (c == mExitCommand) {
                destroyApp(false);
                notifyDestroyed();
              }
              else if (c == mFindCommand) {
                // Show the progress form.
                mDisplay.setCurrent(mProgressForm);
                // Do the query.
                String word = mSubmitBox.getString();
                Poster p = new Poster(word);
                p.start(); // Runs in its own thread.
              }
            }

            public class Poster extends Thread {
              private static final String kURL = "http://www.dict.org/bin/Dict";
              private static final String kParameters =
                  "Form=Dict1&Strategy=*&Database=jargon&Query=";

              private String mPostString;

              public Poster(String word) {
                mPostString = kParameters + word;
              }

              public void run() {
                HttpConnection c = null;
                InputStream in = null;
                OutputStream out = null;
                StringBuffer definition = new StringBuffer();

                try {
                  mProgressString.setText("Sending...");
                  c = (HttpConnection)Connector.open(kURL);

                  // Set the request method and headers
                  c.setRequestMethod(HttpConnection.POST);
                  c.setRequestProperty("User-Agent",
                      "Profile/MIDP-1.0 Configuration/CLDC-1.0");
                  c.setRequestProperty("Content-Language", "en-US");
                  c.setRequestProperty("Content-Type",
                      "application/x-www-form-urlencoded");
                  c.setRequestProperty("Content-Length",
                      String.valueOf(mPostString.length()));
```

```
      // Write out the POST parameters.
      out = c.openOutputStream();
      out.write(mPostString.getBytes());
      out.flush();

      mProgressString.setText("Waiting...");
      in = c.openInputStream();

      String line;
      int count = 0;
      boolean inPre = false;
      while ((line = readLine(in)) != null) {
        count++;
        mProgressGauge.setValue(count % 10);
        mProgressString.setText("Receiving");
        int preIndex = line.indexOf("<pre>");
        int slashpreIndex = line.indexOf("</pre>");
        if (preIndex != -1)
          inPre = true;
        else if (slashpreIndex != -1)
          inPre = (preIndex > slashpreIndex);
        else if (inPre == true)
          trimAndAppend(line, definition);
      }
    }
    catch (IOException ioe) {
      Alert error = new Alert("Error", ioe.toString(), null, null);
      mDisplay.setCurrent(error, mSubmitBox);
    }
    finally {
      try {
        if (in != null)
          in.close();
        if (out != null)
          out.close();
        if (c != null)
          c.close();
      }
      catch (IOException ioe) {}
    }
    Alert results = new Alert("Definition", definition.toString(),
        null, null);
    results.setTimeout(Alert.FOREVER);
    mDisplay.setCurrent(results, mSubmitBox);
}
```

```
    private byte[] mBuffer = new byte[512];

    protected String readLine(InputStream in) throws IOException {
      int c, index = 0;
      while ((c = in.read()) != -1 && c != '\n')
        mBuffer[index++] = (byte)c;
      if (c == -1 && index == 0)
        return null;
      return new String(mBuffer, 0, index);
    }

    protected void trimAndAppend(String line, StringBuffer amalgam) {
      boolean leading = true;
      boolean inTag = false;

      int c;
      for (int i = 0; i < line.length(); i++) {
        c = line.charAt(i);
        if (c == '<')
          inTag = true;
        else if (c == '>')
          inTag = false;
        else if (c == ' ' && leading == true)
          ;
        else if (inTag == false) {
          amalgam.append((char)c);
          leading = false;
        }
      }
      if (leading == false) amalgam.append(' ');
    }
  }
}
```

Compiling a MIDlet

Writing MIDlets is an example of cross-compiling, where you compile code on
one platform and run it on another. In this case, you'll be compiling a MIDlet
using J2SE on your desktop computer. The MIDlet itself will run on a mobile
phone, pager, or other mobile information device that supports the MIDP.

Normally, when you're compiling source code, the CLASSPATH environment variable points to all the classes that your source code needs to know about. When you use javac to compile a file, there are some implied APIs that get included, like the classes in java.lang. With MIDlets, however, the situation is a little more complicated. Say that you use the java.lang.System class in your MIDlet. How do you let the compiler know that you want to use the MIDP version of this class, not the J2SE version?

The answer is a command line option, -bootclasspath. This option lets you point to a classpath that describes the fundamental APIs against which you will be compiling your source code. In our case, this option should be used to specify the *classes* directory in the MIDP reference implementation installation. On the command line, it looks like this:

```
javac -bootclasspath \midp\classes Jargoneer.java
```

(You will need to adjust the path to *classes* if you installed the MIDP software in a different location.)

Try this at the command line. The compiler will attempt to compile your source code, referencing the MIDP classes as needed. Fix up any errors you might have until it compiles.

If you're using the J2ME Wireless Toolkit, you don't have to worry about the details of -bootclasspath. Start up the toolkit, called **KToolbar**. Choose **New Project...** from the toolbar, and create a new project. J2MEWTK asks you for the name of the project and the MIDlet class name; use "Jargoneer" for both. J2MEWTK represents projects as subdirectories of the *apps* directory. The following diagram shows the contents of the *Jargoneer* directory after the new project is created.

```
<J2MEWTK directory>
    apps
        example
        Jargoneer
            bin
            classes
            res
            src
            tmpclasses
        UIDemo
    bin
    doc
    lib
    nojam
```

Save the source code for Jargoneer in the project's *src* directory. You can simply click the **Build** button in the J2MEWTK tool bar to compile the open project.

Preverifying Class Files

Now comes an entirely new step in building your program, *preverifying*. Because the memory on small devices is so scarce, the MIDP (actually, the CLDC) specifies that bytecode verification be split into two pieces. Somewhere off the device, a preverify step is performed. The device itself is only required to do a lightweight second verification step before loading classes.

As you may recall, bytecode verification is one of the foundation stones of Java's runtime security model. Before a classloader dynamically loads a class, the bytecode verifier checks the class file to make sure it behaves well and won't do nasty things to the JVM. Unfortunately, the code that implements the bytecode verifier is bulky, too large to fit on a small device like a mobile phone. The two-step bytecode verification dictated by the CLDC works like this:

1. Off the device, class files are preverified. Certain checks are performed, and the class file is massaged into a format that the lightweight second-step verifier can easily handle.

2. On the device, the second step of verification is performed as classes are loaded. If a class file has not been preverified, it is rejected.

The MIDP software contains a tool called preverify that performs the first step. On Windows, using Sun's reference implementation, this tool is buried in the *build\win32\tools* directory in the MIDP installation directory. You may wish to add it to your path.

The preverify tools takes, as input, a class file. It produces a preverified class file. You need to specify a classpath, so the tool can find the class you want to preverify as well as any referenced classes. Finally, you can specify an output directory using the -d option. To overwrite an existing class file with a preverified version, you could do something like this:

```
preverify -classpath .;\midp\classes -d . Jargoneer
```

Don't forget that Jargoneer has an inner class, Poster, which must also be preverified:

```
preverify -classpath .;\midp\classes -d . Jargoneer$Poster
```

In these examples, the -d option tells `preverify` to write the preverified class file to the current directory.

If you're using the J2MEWTK instead of the command-line tools, you don't have to worry about explicitly preverifying your class files. The J2MEWTK preverifies class files automatically.

> **NOTE** *Splitting bytecode verification into two pieces like this has important security ramifications. Devices should only download code from trusted sources, using a secure method, because some bytecode verification is performed off the device. An attacker could supply malicious code that appeared to be preverified, even if it violated the rules of the full J2SE bytecode verifier. To the MIDP second-step verifier, the code would look okay.*

Sun's MIDP Emulator

Sun's MIDP reference implementation includes an emulator named `midp`. It emulates an imaginary MID, a mobile telephone with some standard keys and a 98×130-pixel screen. The J2MEWTK includes an almost identical emulator, as well as a pager emulator.

Running MIDlets

Once you've got a preverified class file, you can use the `midp` emulator to run it. The emulator is an application that runs under J2SE that acts just like a MID. It shows itself on your screen as a representative device, a generic mobile phone. You can run your MIDlet by typing the following at the command line, assuming you added *midp\bin* to your PATH:

```
midp Jargoneer
```

Or, if you're using the J2MEWTK, you can simply choose an emulator from the Device combo box and click the **Run** button to fire up the emulator.

If all goes well, you'll see something like the window shown in Figure 2-1. Congratulations! You've just built and run your first MIDlet.

Using the Emulator Controls

The J2MEWTK emulator appears as a generic mobile phone, as shown in Figure 2-1.

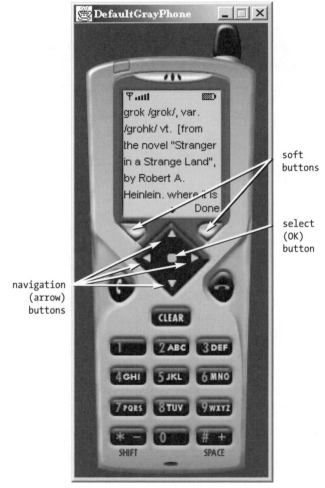

Figure 2-1. Buttons on the mobile phone emulator

Sun's J2MEWTK emulator exhibits several qualities that you are likely to find in real devices:

- The device has a small screen size and limited input capabilities.

- Two *soft buttons* are available. A soft button does not have a fixed function. Generally, the function of the button at any given time is shown on the screen near the button. In MIDlets, the soft buttons are used for commands.

- *Navigation buttons* are provided to allow the user to browse through lists or other sets of choices.

- A *select button* allows the user to make a choice after moving to it with the navigation buttons. (Think "Yes, that's my final answer.")

Environment Variables

The emulator included with Sun's MIDP reference implementation can be controlled via environment variables. One of the most interesting ones is SCREEN_DEPTH, which determines the bit depth of the emulator's screen. Possible values are shown in Table 2-1.

Table 2-1. SCREEN_DEPTH *Values*

VALUE	MEANING
1	Black and white
2	Grayscale, 4 levels
4	Grayscale, 16 levels
8	Color, 256 colors

SCREEN_DEPTH and the other environment variables that can be used are documented in the *docs\midp-env.html* installed in the reference implementation directory.

The Wireless Toolkit Devices

The J2MEWTK includes the four device emulators that follow:

- DefaultColorPhone is basically the emulator shown in Figure 2-1 with a screen depth of 8. The screen measures 98 × 130 pixels.

- DefaultGrayPhone is the same emulator with a screen depth of 4.

- MinimumPhone is a stripped-down mobile phone with a 96 × 54-pixel screen, the smallest allowed by the MIDP specification.

- Pager is a generic pager.

You can easily switch to a different emulator by choosing it from the Device combo box.

Tour of MIDP Features

Having gotten our first MIDlet to run, let's take a moment to admire it. There are several salient features, even in such a small example.

It's Java

First of all, Jargoneer is written in the Java language, the same language you'd use to code servlets, Enterprise JavaBeans, or J2SE client applications. If you're already a J2SE developer, you'll be extremely comfortable developing MIDlets.

Not only is the Java language familiar, but also many core APIs are very similar to J2SE. Notice, for example, that multithreading in Jargoneer is just the same as it might be in any other Java code. The inner class Poster extends java.lang.Thread, and kicking off a new thread is the same as it always was:

```
Poster p = new Poster(word);
p.start(); // Runs in its own thread.
```

Significant parts of java.lang are essentially unchanged from J2SE, as are parts of java.io and java.util. Lots of the Jargoneer source code involves parsing the word definition received back from the Jargon File server, and this should all be very familiar stream handling and string manipulation.

MIDlet Life Cycle

Jargoneer also demonstrates the basic structure of MIDlets. Like all good MIDlets, it extends javax.microedition.midlet.MIDlet, the base class for all MIDP applications. Special software on the device, called the Java Application Manager (JAM) or MIDlet management software controls the process of installing, running, and removing MIDlets. When a user chooses to run your MIDlet, it is the JAM that creates an instance of the MIDlet class and runs methods on it.

The sequence of methods that will be called in your MIDlet subclass is defined by the MIDlet life cycle. MIDlets, like applets and servlets, have a small set of well-defined states. The JAM will call methods in the MIDlet to signify changes from one state to another. You can see these methods in Jargoneer: startApp(), pauseApp(), destroyApp(), and Jargoneer's constructor are all part of the MIDlet life cycle.

Generalized User Interface

Jargoneer's user-interface code may take you by surprise. Later on, we'll spend several chapters on user interface. For now, the important thing to notice is how Jargoneer's user interface is flexible enough to run on devices with different screen sizes and different input capabilities. A big part of MIDP's appeal, after all, is the concept of writing one set of source code that runs on multiple devices.

One example of MIDP's generalized user interface is the TextBox that is initially shown when Jargoneer is launched. Figure 2-2 shows this TextBox.

Figure 2-2. The Jargoneer's TextBox

TextBox is a text input field. It has a title and an area for entering text. It has a simple design and can easily be shown on screens of different sizes. Even more interesting are the commands that appear at the bottom of the TextBox. These are Exit and Find. The code that creates the TextBox and its commands is in Jargoneer's constructor:

```
mExitCommand = new Command("Exit", Command.EXIT, 0);
mFindCommand = new Command("Find", Command.SCREEN, 0);
// ...
mSubmitBox = new TextBox("Jargoneer", "", 32, 0);
mSubmitBox.addCommand(mExitCommand);
mSubmitBox.addCommand(mFindCommand);
mSubmitBox.setCommandListener(this);
```

Notice how the commands are created. We specify only a label and a type, and we register an event listener to find out when the commands are invoked. This is all purposely vague—it leaves the implementation considerable latitude in deciding how commands should be displayed and invoked. In Sun's J2MEWTK emulator, for example, TextBox shows its commands at the bottom of the screen and allows the user to invoke them using soft buttons. Another device might put both commands in a menu and allow the user to invoke them using a selector wheel or some other mechanism.

The Likelihood of Server-Side Components

The Jargoneer example connects to a Web server, sends a request, and receives a response. Unfortunately, we're receiving a lot of information we don't need. We go to considerable trouble in the Poster class to parse through the returned HTML response to extract the definition we want. Architecturally, it looks like Figure 2-3.

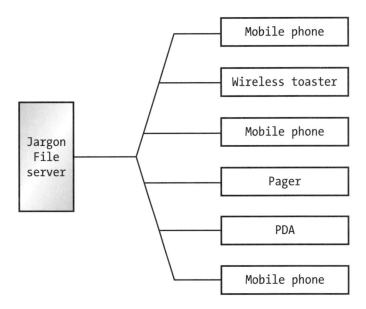

Figure 2-3. Jargoneer *architecture*

A much more likely architecture is shown in Figure 2-4.

Instead of hitting the Web server directly from our code, we go through a different server. This server actually queries the Jargon File, parses the result, and returns the definition to the device in some stripped-down format. This is advantageous from several standpoints:

- Bandwidth is expensive in terms of both time and money. Today's wireless networks are relatively slow, so less data passing through the air means less waiting time for your users. Also, wireless service tends to be pricey, so less data passing through the air means smaller bills for your users.

- Small devices have limited memory and processing power. It is unwise to spend these limited resources on tasks like parsing HTML. In general, you will be able to place most of the processing burden of your application on a server component, making your client MIDlet's life very easy.

- In this particular application, the HTML parsing is not very stable. Suppose the server we are using decides to return its Jargon File definitions in a different format; if four million users are running Jargoneer, then four million copies of our code have just broken. Performing this task on a server gives it a single point of failure and a single point of update. If we fix the parsing code on the server, the interface between the server and the client devices can remain unchanged. This makes it easy to upgrade or fix Jargoneer.

Network MIDP applications are likely to need a server component. If you're planning to do much MIDP development, you might like to study up on Java servlets.

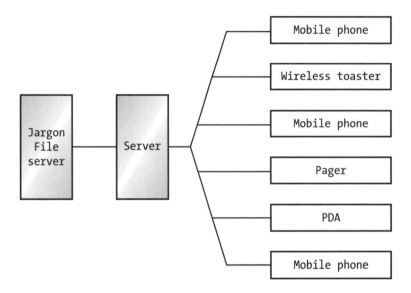

Figure 2-4. A cleaner architecture for Jargoneer

Packaging Your Application

You won't pass class files directly to a MID to deploy an application. Instead, you'll package them in a Java Archive (JAR) using the jar tool that comes with the Java 2 SDK.

If you're using the J2ME Wireless Toolkit, you won't ever have to perform these steps manually; the toolkit automatically packages your MIDlets. Nevertheless, you might want to read through this section so you understand exactly what's going on.

If you're using the MIDP reference implementation, you should follow these steps to package your MIDlets.

We'll only sketch the steps here; in the next chapter you'll learn all the gory details of MIDlets and MIDlet suites.

Manifest Information

Every JAR includes a manifest file, *META-INF\MANIFEST.MF*, that describes the contents of the archive. For MIDlet JARs, the manifest file should contain extra information. The extra information is stuff that's important to the MIDP runtime environment, like the MIDlet's class name and the versions of CLDC and MIDP that the MIDlet expects.

You can specify extra manifest information in a simple text file and tell the jar utility to include that information in the manifest when the JAR is created. To package Jargoneer, for example, save the following text in a file named *extra.mf*:

```
MIDlet-1: Jargoneer, , Jargoneer
MIDlet-Name: Jargoneer
MIDlet-Vendor: Sun Microsystems
MIDlet-Version: 1.0
MicroEdition-Configuration: CLDC-1.0
MicroEdition-Profile: MIDP-1.0
```

Now assemble the MIDlet classes and the extra manifest information into a JAR with the following command:

```
jar cvmf extra.mf Jargoneer.jar Jargoneer.class Jargoneer$Poster.class
```

With J2MEWTK, the toolkit automatically assembles your application into a MIDlet suite JAR when you press the **Build** button. It's very convenient, and it saves you from the effort of learning the jar tool.

Creating a MIDlet Descriptor

One additional file is needed before your MIDlet is ready to go out the door. An *application descriptor* file must be created. This file contains a lot of the same information that's in the MIDlet JAR manifest file. However, it lives outside the JAR and enables application management software to learn about a MIDlet JAR without installing it.

The application descriptor is a text file with a .jad extension. Type in the following and save it as `Jargoneer.jad`:

```
MIDlet-1: Jargoneer, , Jargoneer
MIDlet-Jar-Size: 3853
MIDlet-Jar-URL: Jargoneer.jar
MIDlet-Name: Jargoneer
MIDlet-Vendor: Sun Microsystems
MIDlet-Version: 1.0
```

The MIDlet descriptor is automatically generated when you press the **Build** button in the J2MEWTK. If you're using the J2MEWTK, you won't need to create the application descriptor yourself.

Running the Packaged Application

If you're using the MIDP reference implementation, you'll need to use some command options to tell the `midp` emulator about your application descriptor and MIDlet JAR:

```
C:\>midp -descriptor Jargoneer.jad -classpath Jargoneer.jar
```

Or, in the J2MEWTK, just select the emulator you want and press the **Run** button.

Running on a Real Device

As of this writing, Motorola has released two MIDP-compliant phones, the i85s and the i50sx, with service provided by Nextel. Although these phones have a MIDP implementation, Nextel is still futzing around with their network. Full HTTP connectivity won't be available until the third quarter of 2001.

How do you actually put MIDlets on the phone? Eventually, of course, MIDlet suites can be downloaded over the network, but the infrastructure hasn't been set up yet. For now, MIDlet suites can be downloaded to Motorola's phones from your desktop computer using a serial cable. You'll need a downloader program on your PC, available here: `http://developer.nextel.com/`. You can buy the phones and the serial cable from Nextel: `http://www.nextel.com/`.

Summary

This chapter took you on a tour of MIDP development. Creating source code is much the same as in J2SE development, but the build process is different. First, the source code must be compiled against the MIDP classes using `javac`'s `-bootclasspath` option. Second, the class files must be preverified using the `preverify` command line tool. With the J2ME Wireless Toolkit (J2MEWTK), these steps are conveniently automated. Just press the **Build** button to build and preverify. Applications can be easily tested in emulators using the J2MEWTK.

CHAPTER 3

All About MIDlets

In Chapter 2, you got a quick introduction to the process of building and running MIDlets. In this chapter, we'll explore the details. We'll cover the subjects that we skimmed in last chapter, starting with the MIDlet life cycle and continuing through to a full discussion of MIDlet packaging.

The MIDlet Life Cycle

MIDP applications are represented by instances of the `javax.microedition.midlet.MIDlet` class. MIDlets have a specific life cycle, which is reflected in the methods and behavior of the `MIDlet` class.

A piece of device software outside the realm of Java, the *application manager*, controls the installation and execution of MIDlets. A MIDlet is installed by moving its class files to a device. The class files will be packaged in a Java Archive (JAR), while an accompanying descriptor file (with a .jad extension) describes the contents of the JAR.

A MIDlet goes through the following states:

1. When the MIDlet is about to be run, an instance is created. The MIDlet's constructor is run, and the MIDlet is in the *Paused* state.

2. Next, the MIDlet enters the *Active* state after the application manager calls `startApp()`.

3. While the MIDlet is Active, the application manager can suspend its execution by calling `pauseApp()`. This puts the MIDlet back in the Paused state. A MIDlet can place itself in the Paused state by calling `notifyPaused()`.

4. The application manager can terminate the execution of the MIDlet by calling `destroyApp()`, at which point the MIDlet is *Destroyed* and patiently awaits garbage collection. A MIDlet can destroy itself by calling `notifyDestroyed()`.

Figure 3-1 shows the states of a MIDlet and the transitions between them.

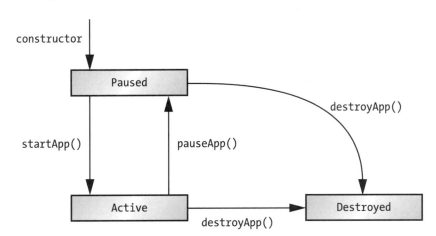

Figure 3-1. MIDlet life cycle

There is one additional method in the MIDlet class related to the MIDlet life cycle: resumeRequest(). A MIDlet in the Paused state can call this method to signal to the application manager that it wants to become Active. It might seem weird to think about a MIDlet in the Paused state running any code at all. However, Paused MIDlets are still able to handle timer events or other types of callbacks and thus have some chances to call resumeRequest(). If the application manager does decide to move a MIDlet from the Paused to the Active state, it will do so through the normal mechanism of calling startApp().

Packaging MIDlets

MIDlets are deployed in *MIDlet suites*. A MIDlet suite is a collection of MIDlets with some extra information; it is composed of two files. One is an *application descriptor*, which is a simple text file. The other is a JAR file that contains the class files and resource files that make up your MIDlet suite. Like any JAR file, a MIDlet suite's JAR file has a manifest file. Figure 3-2 shows a diagram of a MIDlet suite.

Packaging a MIDlet suite consists of three steps:

1. The class files and resource files that make up the MIDlets are packaged into a JAR file. Usually, you'll use the jar command line tool to accomplish this.

2. Additional information that's needed at runtime is placed in the JAR's manifest file. All JARs include a manifest; a MIDlet suite JAR contains some extra information needed by application management software.

3. An application descriptor file must also be generated. This is a file with a
   .jad extension that describes the MIDlet suite JAR. It can be used by the
   application management software to decide whether a MIDlet suite JAR
   should be downloaded to the device.

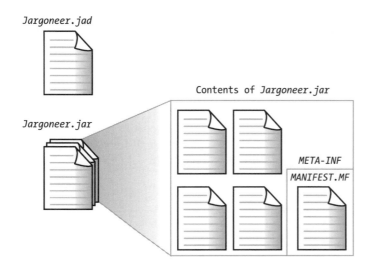

Figure 3-2. Anatomy of a MIDlet suite

MIDlet Manifest Information

The information stored in a MIDlet's manifest file consists of name and value
pairs, like a properties file. For example, an unadorned JAR manifest might look
like this:

```
Manifest-Version: 1.0
Created-By: 1.3.0 (Sun Microsystems Inc.)
```

The MIDlet JAR manifest for Jargoneer looks like this:

```
Manifest-Version: 1.0
MIDlet-1: Jargoneer, Jargoneer.png, Jargoneer
MIDlet-Name: Jargoneer
MIDlet-Version: 1.0
MIDlet-Vendor: Sun Microsystems
Created-By: 1.3.0 (Sun Microsystems Inc.)
MicroEdition-Configuration: CLDC-1.0
MicroEdition-Profile: MIDP-1.0
```

The extra attributes describe software versions, class names, and other information about the MIDlet suite. The following attributes must be included:

MIDlet-Name: Despite the moniker, this attribute actually refers to the name of the entire MIDlet suite, not just one MIDlet.

MIDlet-Version: This describes the version of the MIDlet suite. It's a number you pick yourself in the form *major.minor.micro.*

MIDlet-Vendor: This is your name or the name of your company.

MIDlet-*n*: For each MIDlet in the MIDlet suite, the displayable name, icon file, and class name are listed. The MIDlets should be numbered starting from 1 and counting up. For example, several MIDlets in a single MIDlet suite could be listed like this:

```
MIDlet-1: Sokoban, /icons/Sokoban.png, example.sokoban.Sokoban
MIDlet-2: Tickets, /icons/Auction.png, example.lcdui.TicketAuction
MIDlet-3: Colors, /icons/ColorChooser.png, example.chooser.Color
MIDlet-4: Stock, /icons/Stock.png, example.stock.StockMIDlet
```

MicroEdition-Configuration: This attribute describes the J2ME configuration required to run the MIDlet suite. For MIDP 1.0 suites, this will always be CLDC-1.0.

MicroEdition-Profile: This describes the profile required by this MIDlet suite. For MIDP 1.0 applications, this is MIDP-1.0.

In addition to the required manifest attributes, the following attributes may also be defined:

MIDlet-Description: The description of the MIDlet suite goes in this attribute.

MIDlet-Icon: Icons for individual MIDlets are described in the MIDlet-*n* attributes. This attribute specifies an icon to represent the entire MIDlet suite.

MIDlet-Info-URL: If additional information about the MIDlet suite is available online, use this attribute to list the URL.

MIDlet-Data-Size: If you know how many bytes of persistent data are required by the MIDlet suite, you can specify the number with this attribute.

> **TIP** *Don't get tripped up by the attribute names. Many of them appear to refer to a single MIDlet, like MIDlet-Name and MIDlet-Description. In fact, these attributes describe an entire MIDlet suite. The only attribute that applies to a specific MIDlet is the MIDlet-n attribute, which is used to list each MIDlet in the suite.*

Application Descriptor

The attributes in a MIDlet suite JAR are used by the application management software to run MIDlets within a suite. The application descriptor, by contrast, contains information that helps a device decide whether or not to load a MIDlet suite. Because an application descriptor is a file separate from the MIDlet suite JAR, it is easy for a device to load and examine the file before downloading the MIDlet suite.

As it happens, a lot of the information in the application descriptor is the same as the information that's in the MIDlet suite JAR. For example, the application descriptor must contain the MIDlet-Name, MIDlet-Version, and MIDlet-Vendor attributes. In addition, it should include the following:

MIDlet-Jar-URL: This is the URL where the MIDlet suite JAR can be found.

MIDlet-Jar-Size: This is the size, in bytes, of the MIDlet suite JAR.

The application descriptor can optionally contain the MIDlet-Description, MIDlet-Icon, MIDlet-Info-URL, and MIDlet-Data-Size attributes.

MIDlet Properties

There's one other possibility for attributes in the manifest or application descriptor. You can add attributes that have meaning to your MIDlets. MIDlets can retrieve the values of these attributes using the `getAppProperty()` in the `javax.microedition.midlet.MIDlet` class. An attribute can be listed in the application descriptor, JAR manifest, or both; if it is listed in both, the value from the application descriptor will be used. In general, it makes sense to store application properties in the application descriptor file. Because it's distinct from the MIDlet suite JAR, the application descriptor can easily be changed to modify the behavior of your MIDlets. You might, for example, store a URL or other configuration information in the application descriptor.

For example, suppose you put an application-specific attribute in the application descriptor, like this:

```
jargoneer.url: http://www.dict.org/bin/Dict
```

Inside the MIDlet, you can retrieve the value of the attribute like this:

```
String url = getAppProperty("jargoneer.url");
```

Changing the URL is as easy as changing the application descriptor, a simple text file. None of your code needs to be recompiled. This could be useful if you were expecting to distribute many copies of a MIDlet and wanted to share the server load among a group of servers. You could distribute the same MIDlet suite JAR with a group of different application descriptors, each one using a MIDlet attribute to point to a different server.

Summary

MIDP applications are called MIDlets. Like applets or servlets, MIDlets have a specific life cycle; they are managed by device software. This chapter detailed the entries that may be in the MIDlet suite manifest file and the application descriptor. Application properties can be used as a way to store information in the application descriptor instead of hard-coding values into the MIDlet source code.

CHAPTER 4

Almost the
Same Old Stuff

As I discussed in Chapter 1, one of the reasons you might be interested in MIDP as a platform is that it's based on the Java programming language and the Java APIs. You'll also recall that MIDP is built on top of the Connected, Limited Device Configuration (CLDC). The CLDC contains most of the APIs that will look familiar to experienced Java programmers.

In this chapter, we'll explore the `java.lang`, `java.io`, and `java.util` packages as defined in the CLDC and MIDP. I'll assume you're already familiar with the basic APIs of J2SE; we'll walk through what's the same and what's different.

No Floating Point

One overarching change is that CLDC does not support floating-point types at all. That means there are no `float` or `double` primitive types. The corresponding wrapper types, `java.lang.Float` and `java.lang.Double`, have also been eliminated.

Floating point support is absent in CLDC because most small devices don't have hardware support for floating-point operations. If calculations involving fractional numbers are important to your application, you can perform them in software. One implementation (using fixed-point integers) can be found at `http://home.rochester.rr.com/ohommes/MathFP/`.

java.lang

Table 4-1 lists the classes and interfaces of `java.lang` in both J2SE (SDK version 1.3) and CLDC/MIDP. Keep in mind that just because a class is listed in the CLDC/MIDP column, it may not have the same API as its J2SE counterpart.

Table 4-1. The java.lang *Package*

INTERFACES

J2SE	*MIDP*
Cloneable	-
Comparable	-
Runnable	Runnable

CLASSES

J2SE	*MIDP*
Boolean	Boolean
Byte	Byte
Character	Character
Character.Subset	-
Character.UnicodeBlock	-
Class	Class
ClassLoader	-
Compiler	-
Double	-
Float	-
InheritableThreadLocal	-
Integer	Integer
Long	Long
Math	Math
Number	-
Object	Object
Package	-
Process	-
Runtime	Runtime
RuntimePermission	-
SecurityManager	-
Short	Short
StrictMath	-
String	String
StringBuffer	StringBuffer
System	System
Thread	Thread
ThreadGroup	-
ThreadLocal	-
Throwable	Throwable
Void	-

`java.lang.Object`, as always, is the root of every Java class. It remains mostly unchanged from J2SE, but there are some important differences.

No User Classloading

As I discussed in Chapter 1, one of the strengths of the Java platform is the ability to load classes at runtime. Unfortunately, because of resource constraints, CLDC/MIDP does not allow you to define your own classloaders. The application manager that runs MIDlets has a classloader, but you cannot access it or use it yourself in any way.

No Object Finalization

Object finalization is not available in CLDC (and, by extension, MIDP). Finalization is a mechanism by which objects can clean up after themselves just before they are garbage collected. In J2SE, an `Object`'s `finalize()` method is called before the object is reclaimed by the garbage collector. No such mechanism exists in the CLDC. If you need to clean up resources, you will need to do it explicitly instead of placing cleanup code in `finalize()`. This is a good idea anyhow, particularly in a small device with limited resources. Explicitly cleaning up resources means that the memory and processing power they consume will be reclaimed sooner rather than later. Cleanup code in `finalize()` methods doesn't get executed until the garbage collector runs, and you never know exactly when that's going to happen.

No Reflection

The CLDC does not support the Reflection API. The target devices of CLDC/MIDP are simply too small to allow it. Although most developers don't need to use reflection directly, it has some important implications. Without reflection, no Remote Method Invocation (RMI) is possible. Without RMI, JINI is not possible. Therefore, CLDC/MIDP implementations cannot run JINI. If you want to run JINI, you'll need to investigate one of the larger J2ME profiles, most likely the RMI Profile or Personal Profile (see Chapter 1).

No Native Methods

Native methods are not supported in CLDC (and, by extension, MIDP). The specification does not support a way to write native device methods and access them from Java.

Multithreading

Using threads is much as you remember it from J2SE, as long as you keep things simple. Creating new threads, starting them, and using the handy java.lang.Runnable interface are the same as in J2SE. One important omission is the interrupt() method, which is not present in CLDC's java.lang.Thread class.

The pause(), resume(), and stop() methods (which are deprecated in J2SE SDK 1.3) are also absent. Thread groups and daemon threads are not supported in CLDC/MIDP; thread naming is also unsupported.

String *and* StringBuffer

Both String and StringBuffer are present in CLDC java.lang package. They are largely unchanged from their J2SE counterparts.

The largest change in the String class is the elimination of valueOf() static methods that convert between floating-point primitives and Strings. A few other obscure methods are absent from CLDC's String class, but you probably won't miss them. For example, although CLDC's String includes the compareTo(String str) method, it doesn't have either the compareTo(Object o) or compareToIgnoreCase(String str) methods that are found in J2SE SDK 1.3.

StringBuffer's append() and insert() methods do not include overrides for floating-point types in the CLDC version of the class. Also, the substring() method has been pruned. Other than that, however, StringBuffer should be very familiar for seasoned J2SE programmers.

Math

The Math class contains static methods for performing mathematical calculations. In J2SE, many of these methods involve trigonometric functions on floating-point numbers. In CLDC, these are all gone, leaving only a handful of methods:

```
public final class Math
    extends java.lang.Object {
  // Static methods
  public static int abs(int a);
  public static long abs(long a);
  public static int max(int a, int b);
  public static long max(long a, long b);
  public static int min(int a, int b);
  public static long min(long a, long b);
}
```

Runtime *and* System

Runtime and System provide access to the Java Virtual Machine and system-wide resources. These two classes are greatly reduced from their J2SE counterparts, so much so that it makes sense to reproduce their entire public API here. First, let's take a look at Runtime:

```
public class Runtime
    extends java.lang.Object {
  // Static methods
  public static Runtime getRuntime();

  // Methods
  public void exit(int status);
  public native long freeMemory();
  public native void gc();
  public native long totalMemory();
}
```

To get the single Runtime instance, call getRuntime(). You can tell the JVM to run its garbage collector (gc()) or shut down (exit()). The other two methods, totalMemory() and freeMemory(), allow you to examine the amount of memory that is available for your application's data.

Note that Runtime does not support running external processes with the exec() method. MIDlets cannot step outside the bounds of the JVM.

System provide static methods for performing various common tasks:

```
public final class System
    extends java.lang.Object {
  // Constants
  public static final PrintStream err;
  public static final PrintStream out;

  // Static methods
  public static native void arraycopy(Object src, int src_position,
      Object dst, int dst_position, int length);
  public static native long currentTimeMillis();
  public static void exit(int status);
  public static void gc();
  public static String getProperty(String key);
  public static native int identityHashCode(Object x);

}
```

The first thing you might notice is that while the err and out PrintStreams are defined, there is no System.in. This makes sense—System.in represents the console input; on a MID, there really isn't any console. In fact, it may seem weird to have System.out and System.err defined. If you print information to System.out, it may not come out anywhere on a device; however, on a device emulator, you may be able to view System.out in a console window.

The gc() and exit() methods are shortcuts for calling the corresponding methods in the Runtime class.

All of System's methods are static. The arraycopy() method provides a fast implementation of array copying. You can access MIDlet properties (described in Chapter 3) using getProperty().

Finally, identityHashCode() is a default used by Object's hashCode() method.

Streams in java.io

The java.io package in the CLDC/MIDP world is a stripped down version of java.io in J2SE. Table 4-2 summarizes the classes of java.io in both J2SE and CLDC/MIDP. As you can see, many of the java.io classes you normally find in J2SE are missing from CLDC/MIDP.

Table 4-2. The java.io Package

INTERFACES	
J2SE	*MIDP*
DataInput	DataInput
DataOutput	DataOutput
Externalizable	-
FileFilter	-
FilenameFilter	-
ObjectInput	-
ObjectInputValidation	-
ObjectOutput	-
ObjectStreamConstants	-
Serializable	-

CLASSES	
J2SE	*MIDP*
BufferedInputStream	-
BufferedOutputStream	-
BufferedReader	-
BufferedWriter	-
ByteArrayInputStream	ByteArrayInputStream
ByteArrayOutputStream	ByteArrayOutputStream
CharArrayReader	-
CharArrayWriter	-

(Continued)

J2SE	MIDP
DataInputStream	DataInputStream
DataOutputStream	DataOutputStream
File	-
FileDescriptor	-
FileInputStream	-
FileOutputStream	-
FilePermission	-
FileReader	-
FileWriter	-
FilterInputStream	-
FilterOutputStream	-
FilterReader	-
FilterWriter	-
InputStream	InputStream
InputStreamReader	InputStreamReader
LineNumberInputStream	-
LineNumberReader	-
ObjectInputStream	-
ObjectInputStream.GetField	-
ObjectOutputStream	-
ObjectOutputStream.PutField	-
ObjectStreamClass	-
ObjectStreamField	-
OutputStream	OutputStream
OutputStreamWriter	OutputStreamWriter
PipedInputStream	-
PipedOutputStream	-
PipedReader	-
PipedWriter	-
PrintStream	PrintStream
PrintWriter	-
PushbackInputStream	-
PushbackReader	-
RandomAccessFile	-
Reader	Reader
SequenceInputStream	-
SerializablePermission	-
StreamTokenizer	-
StringBufferInputStream	-
StringReader	-
StringWriter	-
Writer	Writer

Although the differences between the J2SE and CLDC classes appear large, they can be easily grouped into three categories:

1. As CLDC/MIDP has no conception of a local file system, all the classes having to do with files have been pruned from the java.io package. This includes File, FileInputStream, FileOutputStream, the corresponding Reader and Writer classes, RandomAccessFile, and various supporting classes. If you need to store data persistently on a device, you'll need to use the javax.microedition.rms package API, described in Chapter 7.

2. Object serialization is not supported in CLDC. This means that the Serializable interface and various object stream classes are not present.

3. Finally, J2SE includes a handful of utility stream classes—things you might want someday but shouldn't include on a device with a small amount of memory. These classes include piped streams, pushback streams, sequence streams, line numbering streams, and a few other gems like StreamTokenizer. If you really need one of these in your MIDlet, you can always package it with your application.[1]

Character Encodings

MIDP includes the Reader and Writer character streams for working with Unicode characters. InputStreamReader and OutputStreamWriter handle the conversion between byte streams and character streams, just as in J2SE. An *encoding* determines how translation occurs between byte streams and character streams. A default encoding is used if you don't specify one. You can pass an encoding name to the constructors for InputStreamReader and OutputStreamWriter, if you wish. So far, this is all the same as in J2SE. In MIDP, though, you will likely find many fewer available encodings than in J2SE.

The default encoding for a MIDP implementation can be obtained by calling System.getProperty("microedition.encoding")—by default, ISO8859_1.

Resource Files

As described in Chapter 7, you can retrieve resource files from your MIDlet suite's JAR file. Use the getResourceAsStream() method in Class; it returns an InputStream that you can use as you please.

---

1. A better idea would be to redesign your application so that complicated stream processing isn't necessary on the MID. In general, you should make your server do as much work as possible and your MIDlet do as little as possible.

java.util

MIDP includes only a dozen classes from J2SE's `java.util` package. Many of the missing classes are part of the Collections API, which is too bulky for small devices. Table 4-3 lists the classes and interfaces of `java.util` in both J2SE and CLDC/MIDP.

Table 4-3. The `java.util` *Package*

INTERFACES	
J2SE	*MIDP*
Collection	-
Comparator	-
Enumeration	Enumeration
EventListener	-
Iterator	-
List	-
ListIterator	-
Map	-
Map.Entry	-
Observer	-
Set	-
SortedMap	-
SortedSet	-

CLASSES	
J2SE	*MIDP*
AbstractCollection	-
AbstractList	-
AbstractMap	-
AbstractSequentialList	-
AbstractSet	-
ArrayList	-
Arrays	-
BitSet	-
Enumeration	Enumeration
Collections	-
Date	Date
Dictionary	-
EventObject	-
GregorianCalendar	-
HashMap	-
HashSet	-
Hashtable	Hashtable

(Continued)

J2SE	MIDP
LinkedList	-
ListResourceBundle	-
Locale	-
Observable	-
Properties	-
PropertyPermission	-
PropertyResourceBundle	-
Random	Random
ResourceBundle	-
SimpleTimeZone	-
Stack	Stack
StringTokenizer	-
Timer	Timer
TimerTask	TimerTask
TimeZone	TimeZone
TreeMap	-
TreeSet	-
Vector	Vector
WeakHashMap	-

Collections

Although the full J2SE Collections API is not supported by MIDP, the old familiar Vector and Hashtable classes remain, as well as the lesser-known Stack. If you are familiar with the JDK 1.0 Vector and Hashtable classes, you should have no trouble with them in MIDP.

Timers

MIDP includes the Timer and TimerTask classes that were introduced into J2SE in the 1.3 version of the SDK. This is one of the few examples of J2SE classes that are not included in the CLDC but are included in MIDP.

Timer's API is identical to the J2SE version with one exception. The constructor that specifies whether the thread is a daemon is missing, as daemon threads are not supported in MIDP. The TimerTask API is exactly the same in J2SE SDK 1.3 and MIDP.

Telling Time

J2SE has an impressive array of classes that can be used for specifying dates and times and translating to and from human-readable representations of dates and times. The J2SE time classes have four distinct responsibilities:

- *Points in time* are represented by instances of `java.util.Date`. If you think of time as a line graph, then an instance of `Date` is just a point on the line.

- *Calendars* are used for representing points in time with calendar fields like year, month, and day. If you're using a Gregorian calendar, for example, then you can translate from a single point in time to a set of calendar values like month, day, and hours, minutes, and seconds. In J2SE, `java.util.Calendar` is a parent class for calendars, while the `java.util.GregorianCalendar` class represents the Gregorian calendar system that is familiar to most of the world.

- *Formatting* classes translate between points in time and human-readable strings. In J2SE, `java.text.DateFormat` is the parent for classes that can both generate and parse human-readable strings representing points in time. Formatting classes are very likely to make use of a calendar. For example, a typical `DateFormat` implementation might use a `GregorianCalendar` to translate a point in time to a set of calendar values, which it would then format in a string.

- *Time zone* classes represent the time zones of the world. The calendar and format classes use a time zone to create a localized representation of a particular point in time. In J2SE, `java.util.TimeZone` is the parent class of all time zones, with `java.util.SimpleTimeZone` as a concrete implementation.

Understanding these classes and their interactions is a little tricky, and it's complicated by the fact that it changed considerably between JDK 1.0 and JDK 1.1. The `java.util.Date` class used to have extra functionality in it; although the methods are deprecated, they're still present and may be confusing. Fortunately, you don't have to deal with this in the CLDC/MIDP world.

The situation is somewhat simpler in CLDC/MIDP. There are fewer classes, for one thing, and the `Date` class API has been cleaned up. In MIDP, the four responsibilities we just discussed are assigned to classes as follows:

- *Points in time* are represented by instances of `java.util.Date`, just like before. The `Date` class, in essence, is just a wrapper for a `long` value that indicates the number of milliseconds since midnight on January 1, 1970. (This is a standard way of representing time. It will work for about another 290 million years, so don't worry about another millennium bug.)

- *Calendars* are still represented by instances of `java.util.Calendar`. However, the `GregorianCalendar` class is no longer part of the public API. To get a `Calendar` instance, you can use the `getInstance()` factory method. Chances are you won't need to do this.

- *Formatting* classes are hidden from view in MIDP. One of the user interface classes, `javax.microedition.lcdui.DateField`, can convert a `Date` to a human-readable display, eliminating the need for you to mess around with date formatters yourself. `DateField`, essentially, is a graphic wrapper around a `Date` instance. It also allows the user to edit calendar and clock fields to produce a new `Date` value. See Chapter 6 for a full discussion of `DateField`.

- *Time zone*s are still represented by instances of `java.util.TimeZone`. `TimeZone` offers several static methods for examining the available time zones and getting an instance representing a particular time zone.

Summary

Developers are bombarded with information, and the best developers are the ones that can learn new material fast. Every once in a while, though, something you already know can be used again. This is one of those cases—something you already know about, the J2SE APIs, comes in very handy as you learn MIDP programming. MIDP's `java.lang`, `java.io`, and `java.util` packages contain classes that look and act a lot like the corresponding classes in J2SE.

CHAPTER 5

Creating a User Interface

MIDP applications are built to run on many different devices without modification. This is particularly difficult in the area of user interface; MIDs have screens of all sizes, in grayscale and in color. Furthermore, the input devices on MIDs vary widely in their abilities, from numeric keypads to alphabetic keyboards, soft keys, and even touch screens. The minimum screen size mandated by the MIDP is 96×54 pixels, with at least one bit of color depth.[1] As for input, the MIDP is fairly open-ended: MIDs are expected to have some type of keyboard, or a touch screen, or possibly both.

Given the wide variety of devices that are compliant with the MIDP, there are two ways to create applications that work well on all MIDs:

- *Abstraction*: Specify a user interface in abstract terms, relying on the MIDP implementation to create something concrete. Instead of saying something like, "Display the word 'Next' on the screen above soft button," you say, "Give me a **Next** command somewhere in this interface."

- *Discovery*: The application learns about the device at runtime and tailors the user interface programmatically. You might, for example, find out how big the device's screen was in order to scale your user interface appropriately.

The MIDP APIs support both methods. Abstraction is the preferred method, as it involves less code in your application and more work by the MIDP implementation. In some cases, like games, you need to be more specific about user interface; these types of applications will discover the capabilities of a device and attempt to tailor their behavior appropriately. MIDP's user-interface APIs are designed so that it's easy to mix the two techniques in the same application.

---

1. Color depth is the number of bits that determine the color of a pixel on the screen. One bit allows for two colors (usually black and white). Four bits allows for 16 colors, which could be different levels of gray or a palette of other colors.

The View from the Top

The MIDP contains user-interface classes in the javax.microedition.lcdui package. The MID's display is represented by an instance of the Display class, accessed from a factory method, getDisplay(). Display's main purpose in life is to keep track of what is currently shown, which is an instance of Displayable. If you think of Display as an easel, a Displayable instance is akin to a canvas on that easel.

MIDlets can change the contents of the display by passing Displayable instances to Display's setCurrent() method. This is the basis of a typical MIDlet:

1. Show a Displayable.

2. Wait for input.

3. Decide what Displayable should be next.

4. Repeat.

Displayable has a small family of subclasses that represent various types of user interfaces. Figure 5-1 shows the lineage.

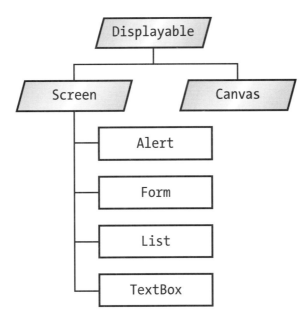

Figure 5-1. Displayables in the javax.microedition.lcdui *package*

`Displayable`'s progeny are split between two branches that correspond to the two methods for creating generalized user interfaces, abstraction and discovery. `Screen` represents displays that are specified in abstract terms. These screens contain standard user-interface items like combo boxes, lists, menus, and buttons. Four subclasses provide a wide range of functionality, as illustrated in Figure 5-2.

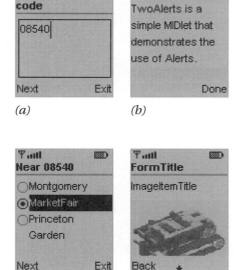

(a)   *(b)*

(c)   *(d)*

Figure 5-2. The four children of `Screen`: *(a)* `TextBox`, *(b)* `Alert`, *(c)* `List`, *and (d)* `Form`

The remainder of this chapter is devoted to explaining the simplest of these four classes, `TextBox` and `Alert`. The next chapter explores the more flexible `List` and `Form`.

For particularly demanding or idiosyncratic displays, you'll have to create a subclass of `Canvas`. Your MIDlet will assume responsibility for most of the drawing, but you get much finer control over what is shown and how user input is handled. `Canvas` supplies methods that allow your MIDlet to learn about its environment—the size of the display, for example, and which kinds of events are supported by the device. User interfaces built on `Canvas` discover the attributes of a device and attempt to create something that looks reasonable. Chapter 9 explains `Canvas`-based user interfaces in detail.

Using Display

There's not much to say about Display, which manages a device's screen. You can get a reference to the device's display by supplying a MIDlet reference to the static getDisplay() method. Typically, you'll do this in the or startApp() method of a MIDlet:

```
public void startApp() {
  Display d = Display.getDisplay(this);
  // ...
}
```

You may be tempted to call getDisplay() in a MIDlet's constructor, but according to the documentation, getDisplay() can only be called after the beginning of the MIDlet's startApp() method.

Once you've got a reference to a device's Display, you'll just need to create something to show (an instance of Displayable) and pass it to one of Display's setCurrent() methods:

```
public void setCurrent(Displayable next)
public void setCurrent(Alert alert, Displayable nextDisplayable)
```

The second version is used when you want to show a temporary message (an Alert) followed by something else. I'll talk more about Alerts at the end of this chapter.

Display's getCurrent() method returns a reference to what's currently being shown.

Finally, you can query a Display to determine what kind of color support it has. The numColors() method returns the number of distinct colors supported by this device, while the isColor() method tells whether the device supports color or grayscale. A Display for a device supporting 16 levels of gray, for example, would return false from isColor() and 16 from numColors().

Event Handling with Commands

Displayable, the parent of all screen displays, supports a very flexible user interface concept, the command. A *command* is something the user can invoke—you can think of it as a button. Like a button, it has a title, like "OK" or "Cancel," and your application can respond appropriately when the user invokes the command. The premise is that you want a command to be available to the user, but you don't really care how it is shown on the screen or exactly how the user invokes it—keypad button, soft button, touch screen, whatever.

Every `Displayable` keeps a list of its `Commands`. You can add and remove `Commands` using the following methods:

```
public void addCommand(Command cmd)
public void removeCommand(Command cmd)
```

Creating `Commands`

In the MIDP, commands are represented by instances of the `Command` class. To create a `Command`, just supply a name, a type, and a priority. The name is usually shown on the screen. The type can be used to signify a commonly used command. It should be one of the values defined in the `Command` class. Table 5-1 shows the type values and their meanings.

Table 5-1. Command Types

NAME	MEANING
OK	Confirms a selection.
CANCEL	Cancels pending changes.
BACK	Moves the user back to a previous screen.
STOP	Stops a running operation.
HELP	Shows application instructions.
SCREEN	Generic type for specific application commands.

To create a standard **OK** command, for example, you would do this:

```
Command c = new Command("OK", Command.OK, 0);
```

To create a command specific to your application, you might do this:

```
Command c = new Command("Launch", Command.SCREEN, 0);
```

It's up to the MIDP implementation to figure out how to show the commands. In the Sun J2MEWTK emulator, commands are assigned to the two soft buttons. A *soft button* is a button on the device keypad with no predefined function, which allows it to serve a different purpose at different times. If there are more commands than there are soft buttons, the commands that don't fit will be grouped into a menu that is assigned to one of the soft buttons.

A simple priority scheme determines who wins when there are more commands than available screen space. Every command has a priority that indicates how hard the display system should try to show the command. Lower numbers indicate a higher priority. If you add a command with priority 0, then several more with priority 1, the priority 0 command will show up on the screen directly. The other commands will most likely end up in a secondary menu.

Responding to Commands

By themselves, Commands aren't very exciting. They'll show up on the screen, but nothing happens automatically when a user invokes a command. An object called a *listener* is notified when the user invokes any command in a Displayable. This follows the basic form of the JavaBeans event model; a Displayable is a *unicast event source*. A Displayable fires off an event every time the user invokes one of its Commands.

The listener is an object that implements the CommandListener interface. To register the listener with a Displayable, use the following method:

```
public void setListener(CommandListener l)
```

Displayable is a unicast event source because it can only have one listener object. (*Multicast* event sources can have multiple listeners and use an add… method for adding listeners rather than a set… method.)

Implementing a CommandListener is a matter of defining a single method:

```
public void commandAction(Command c, Displayable s)
```

When a command is invoked, the Displayable that contains it calls the commandAction() method of the registered listener.

> **TIP**   *Event listeners should not perform lengthy processing inside the event-handling thread. The system uses a thread to call* commandAction() *in response to user input. If your implementation of* commandAction() *does any heavy thinking, it will tie up the system's event-handling thread. If you have anything complicated to do, use a separate thread.*

A Simple Example

By way of illustration, consider the following class:

```
import javax.microedition.midlet.*;
import javax.microedition.lcdui.*;

public class Commander extends MIDlet {
  public void startApp() {
    Displayable d = new TextBox("TextBox", "Commander", 20, 0);
```

```
    Command c = new Command("Exit", Command.EXIT, 0);
    d.addCommand(c);
    d.setCommandListener(new CommandListener() {
      public void commandAction(Command c, Displayable s) {
        notifyDestroyed();
      }
    });

    Display.getDisplay(this).setCurrent(d);
  }

  public void pauseApp() {}

  public void destroyApp(boolean unconditional) {}
}
```

This MIDlet creates a TextBox, which is a kind of Displayable, and adds a single command to it. The listener is created as an anonymous inner subclass. In Sun's J2MEWTK, this MIDlet appears as shown in Figure 5-3.

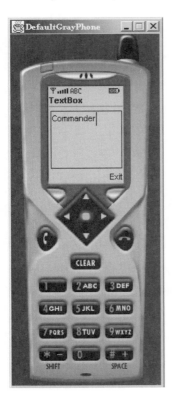

Figure 5-3. A simple MIDlet with a single command, **Exit**

Figure 5-3 shows the **Exit** command being mapped to one of the MIDP simulator's soft buttons. If you add another command to this MIDlet, it will be mapped to the other soft button. If you continue adding commands, the ones that don't fit on the screen will be put into an off-screen menu. For example, a screen with four commands shows up in the MIDP simulator, as illustrated in Figure 5-4a.

If you press the soft button for **Menu**, you'll see the remainder of the commands as shown in Figure 5-4b. Menu items can now be selected by pressing a number or using the arrow keys for navigation. In the example shown in Figure 5-4, the **Exit** command is given a higher priority (lower number) than the other commands, which insures that it appears directly on the screen. The other commands, with a lower priority, are relegated to the command menu.

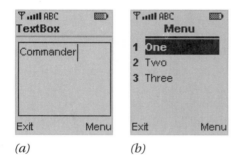

(a)   *(b)*

*Figure 5-4. This MIDlet has more commands than the device has soft buttons. Invoking the (a) system-generated **Menu** command brings up the (b) remaining commands.*

Screens and Tickers

The remainder of this chapter and all of Chapter 6 are devoted to Screen and its subclasses, which is the left branch of the hierarchy shown in Figure 5-1. Screen is the base class for all classes that represent generalized user interfaces.

Canvas, by contrast, is a base class for specialized interfaces, such as those for games. Canvas will be fully covered later, in Chapter 9.

In the coming sections, we'll explore each of Screen's child classes. Here, I'll briefly describe what all Screens have in common: a title and a ticker. The *title* is just what you expect: a string that appears at the top of the screen. A *ticker* is simply a bit of text that scrolls across the top of a Screen, named after old-fashioned stock tickers.

The title is a text string displayed at the top of the screen. As you saw in Figure 5-3, the title of the screen is "TextBox." Subclasses of Screen have constructors that set the title, but the title may also be accessed using the following methods:

```
public void setTitle(String newTitle)
public String getTitle()
```

The ticker is just as easy to access:

```
public void setTicker(Ticker newTicker)
public Ticker getTicker()
```

The Ticker class is a simple wrapper for a string. To add a ticker to a screen, then, you would do something like this:

```
// Screen s = ...
Ticker ticker = new Ticker("This is the ticker message!");
s.setTicker(ticker);
```

Figure 5-5 shows a ticker in action. The full text of the ticker is "A ticker scrolls slowly."

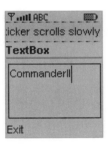

Figure 5-5. A ticker scrolls across the top of a screen.

TextBox, the Simplest Screen

The simplest type of screen is the TextBox, which you've already seen in action. TextBox allows the user to enter a string. Keep in mind that on a garden-variety MID, text input is a tedious process. Many MIDs only have a numeric keypad, so entering a single character is a matter of one, two, or three button presses. A good MIDlet requires minimal user input.

That said, your MIDlet may need some kind of input—perhaps a Zip code, or a short name, or some kind of password. In these cases, you'll probably want to use a TextBox.

A TextBox is created by specifying four parameters:

```
public TextBox(String title, String text, int maxSize, int constraints)
```

The title is used as the screen title, while text and maxSize determine the initial text and maximum size of the text box. Finally, constraints can be to restrict the user's input. Constants from the TextField class are used to specify the type of input required:

- ANY allows any type of input.

- NUMERIC restricts the input to numbers.

- PHONENUMBER requires a telephone number.

- EMAILADDR input must be an e-mail address.

- URL input must be a Web address.

- PASSWORD characters are not shown when entered; generally, they are represented by asterisks.

If you don't want the TextBox to perform any validation, use ANY or its numerical equivalent, 0, for the constraints parameter in the constructor.

The PASSWORD constraint may be combined with any of the other constraints using the OR operator. For example, to create a TextBox that constrained input to an e-mail address but wanted to keep the entered data hidden, you would do something like this:

```
Displayable d = new TextBox("Email", "", 64,
        TextField.EMAILADDR | TextField.PASSWORD);
```

If you think about it, though, PASSWORD is probably more trouble than it's worth. The point of PASSWORD fields, at least on desktop machines, is to keep someone walking past your computer screen from seeing your secret password. For every character you enter, the password field shows an asterisk or some other symbol. As you type your secret password, all that shows up on the screen is a line of asterisks (so casual observers cannot see your password). On mobile phones and other small devices, this is less of a concern, as the screens are smaller and much more difficult to read than a typical desktop monitor.

Furthermore, the difficulty of entering data on a small device means that it will be hard to correctly enter passwords typing blind. Mobile phones, for example, typically require pressing keys several times to enter a single letter. On Sun's J2MEWTK emulator, pressing the '7' key twice enters the letter 'Q.' On a real device, you would have to enter a password "gandalf" with the following sequence of key presses: 4, 2, 6, 6, 3, 2, 5, 5, 5, 3, 3, 3. Without visual feedback, it would be extremely easy to make a mistake when entering a password. ("Did I press the 5 key two times or three times?") The J2MEWTK emulator shows the current character but previously typed characters are shown as asterisks. Good passwords typically have mixed case, numbers, and possibly punctuation; these would be hard to get right.

Using Alerts

An *alert* is an informative message shown to the user. In the MIDP universe, there are two flavors of alert:

- A *timed* alert is shown for a certain amount of time, typically just a few seconds. It displays an informative message that does not need to be acknowledged, like "Your transaction is complete," or "I can't do that right now, Dave."

- A *modal* alert stays up until the user dismisses it. Modal alerts are useful when you need to offer the user a choice of actions. You might display a message like "Are you ready to book these tickets?" and offer **Yes** and **No** commands as options.

MIDP alerts can have an associated icon, like a stop sign or question mark. Alerts may even have an associated sound, although this depends on the implementation. MIDP alerts are very much the same concept as modal dialogs in windowing systems like MacOS and Windows. Figure 5-6 shows a typical Alert.

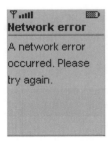

Figure 5-6. Alerts are similar to modal dialogs in a desktop windowing system.

Alerts are represented by instances of the `javax.microedition.lcdui.Alert` class, which offers the following constructors:

```
public Alert()
public Alert(String title, String alertText, Image alertImage, AlertType
alertType)
```

Any or all of the parameters in the second constructor may be `null`.

By default, timed `Alert`s are created using a default timeout value; you can find out the default value by calling `getDefaultTimeout()`. To change the `Alert`'s timeout, call `setTimeout()` with the timeout value in milliseconds. A special value, `FOREVER`, may be used to indicate that the `Alert` is modal.

You could create a simple timed `Alert` with the following code:

```
Alert alert = new Alert("Sorry", "I'm sorry, Dave... ", null, null);
```

To explicitly set the timeout value to five seconds, you could do this:

```
alert.setTimeout(5000);
```

If, instead, you wanted a modal alert, you would use the special value `FOREVER`:

```
alert.setTimeout(Alert.FOREVER);
```

The MIDP implementation will automatically supply a way to dismiss a modal alert. Sun's reference implementation, for example, provides a **Done** command mapped to a soft button.

Alert types serve as hints to the underlying MIDP implementation. The implementation may use the alert type to decide what kind of sound to play when the alert is shown. The `AlertType` class provides five types, accessed as static member variables: `ALARM`, `CONFIRMATION`, `ERROR`, `INFO`, and `WARNING`.

The following example, `TwoAlerts`, shows both types of alerts. It features a main `TextBox` that is displayed when the MIDlet begins. Two commands, **Go** and **About**, provide access to the alerts. The **Go** command shows a timed alert that contains a message about a fictitious network error. The **About** command displays a modal alert that could contain copyright information. A third command, **Exit**, provides a way to exit the MIDlet. Keep in mind that all three commands may not fit on the screen; some of them may be accessible from a secondary menu.

```
import javax.microedition.midlet.*;
import javax.microedition.lcdui.*;
public class TwoAlerts
    extends MIDlet
    implements CommandListener {
  private Display mDisplay;

  private TextBox mTextBox;
  private Alert mTimedAlert;
  private Alert mModalAlert;

  private Command mAboutCommand, mGoCommand, mExitCommand;

  public TwoAlerts() {
    mAboutCommand = new Command("About", Command.SCREEN, 1);
    mGoCommand = new Command("Go", Command.SCREEN, 1);
    mExitCommand = new Command("Exit", Command.EXIT, 2);
  }

  public void startApp() {
    mDisplay = Display.getDisplay(this);
    mTextBox = new TextBox("TwoAlerts", " ", 1, TextField.ANY);
    mTextBox.addCommand(mAboutCommand);
    mTextBox.addCommand(mGoCommand);
    mTextBox.addCommand(mExitCommand);
    mTextBox.setCommandListener(this);

    mTimedAlert = new Alert("Network error",
        "A network error occurred. Please try again.",
        null,
        AlertType.INFO);
    mModalAlert = new Alert("About TwoAlerts",
        "TwoAlerts is a simple MIDlet that demonstrates the use of Alerts.",
        null,
        AlertType.INFO);
    mModalAlert.setTimeout(Alert.FOREVER);

    mDisplay.setCurrent(mTextBox);
  }

  public void pauseApp() {
  }
```

```
      public void destroyApp(boolean unconditional) {}

      public void commandAction(Command c, Displayable s) {
        if (c == mAboutCommand)
          mDisplay.setCurrent(mModalAlert);
        else if (c == mGoCommand)
          mDisplay.setCurrent(mTimedAlert, mTextBox);
        else if (c == mExitCommand)
          notifyDestroyed();
      }
    }
```

Summary

MIDP's main user-interface classes are based on abstractions that can be adapted to devices that have different display and input capabilities. Several varieties of prepackaged screen classes make it easy to create a user interface. Screens have a title and an optional ticker. Most importantly, screens can contain Commands, which the implementation makes available to the user. Your application can respond to commands by acting as a listener object. This chapter described TextBox, a screen for accepting user input, and Alert, a simple screen for displaying information. In the next chapter, we'll get into the more complex List and Form classes.

CHAPTER 6

Lists and Forms

In the last chapter, you learned about MIDP's simpler screen classes. Now we're getting into deeper waters, with screens that show lists and screens with mixed types of controls.

Using Lists

After TextBox and Alert, the next simplest Screen is List, which allows the user to select items (called *elements*) from a list of choices. A text string or an image is used to represent each element in the list. List supports the selection of a single element or of multiple elements.

There are two main types of List, denoted by constants in the Choice interface:

- MULTIPLE designates a list where multiple elements may be selected simultaneously.

- EXCLUSIVE specifies a list where only one element may be selected. It is akin to a group of radio buttons.

Understanding List *Types*

For both MULTIPLE and EXCLUSIVE lists, selection and confirmation are separate steps. In fact, List does not handle confirmation for these types of lists—your MIDlet will need to provide some other mechanism (probably a Command) that allows users to confirm their choices. MULTIPLE lists allow users to select and deselect various elements before confirming the selection. EXCLUSIVE lists permit users to change their minds several times before confirming the selection.

Figure 6-1a shows an EXCLUSIVE list. The user navigates through the list using the arrow up and down keys. An element is selected by pressing the select button on the device. Figure 6-1b shows a MULTIPLE list. It works basically the same way as an EXCLUSIVE list, but multiple elements can be selected simultaneously. As before, the user moves through the list with the up and down arrow keys. The select key toggles the selection of a particular element.

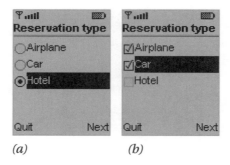

(a)   *(b)*

Figure 6-1. List types: (a) EXCLUSIVE *and (b)* MULTIPLE *lists*

A further refinement of EXCLUSIVE also exists: IMPLICIT lists combine the steps of selection and confirmation. The IMPLICIT list acts just like a menu. Figure 6-2 shows an IMPLICIT list with images and text for each element. When the user hits the select key, the list immediately fires off an event, just like a Command. An IMPLICIT list is just like an EXCLUSIVE list in that the user can only select one of the list elements. But with IMPLICIT lists, there's no opportunity for the user to change his or her mind before confirming the selection.

Figure 6-2. IMPLICIT *lists combine selection and confirmation.*

Event Handling for IMPLICIT Lists

When the user makes a selection in an IMPLICIT List, the commandAction() method of the List's CommandListener is invoked. A special value is passed to commandAction() as the Command parameter:

```
public static final Command SELECT_COMMAND
```

For example, you can test the source of command events like this:

```
public void commandAction(Command c, Displayable s) {
  if (c == nextCommand)
    // ...
  else if (c == List.SELECT_COMMAND)
    // ...
}
```

There's an example at the end of this chapter that demonstrates an IMPLICIT List.

Creating Lists

To create a List, specify a title and a list type. If you have the element names and images available ahead of time, you can pass them in the constructor:

```
public List(String title, int type)
public List(String title, int type, String[] stringElements, Image[]
imageElements)
```

The stringElements parameter cannot be null; however, stringElements or imageElements may contain null array elements. If both the string and image for a given list element are null, the element is displayed blank. If both the string and the image are defined, the element will display using the image and the string.

Some Lists will have more elements than can be displayed on the screen. Indeed, the actual number of elements that will fit varies from device to device. But don't worry: List implementations automatically handle scrolling up and down to show the full contents of the List.

About Images

Our romp through the List class yields a first look at images. Instances of the javax.microedition.lcdui.Image class represent images in the MIDP. The specification dictates that implementations be able to load images files in PNG format.[1] This format supports both a transparent color and animated images.

Image has no constructors, but the Image class offers four createImage() factory methods for obtaining Image instances. The first two are for loading images from PNG data.

---

1. MIDP implementations are not required to recognize all varieties of PNG files. The documentation for the Image class has the specifics.

```
public static Image createImage(String name)
public static Image createImage(byte[] imagedata, int imageoffset,
    int imagelength)
```

The first method attempts to create an Image from the named file, which should be packaged inside the JAR that contains your MIDlet. You should use an absolute pathname or the image file may not be found. The second method creates an Image using data in the supplied array. The data starts at the given array offset, imageoffset, and is imagelength bytes long.

Images may be *mutable* or *immutable*. Mutable Images can be modified by calling getGraphics() and using the returned Graphics object to draw on the image. (For full details on Graphics, see Chapter 9.) If you try to call getGraphics() on an immutable Image, an IllegalStateException will be thrown.

The two createImage() methods described above return immutable Images. To create a mutable Image, use the following method:

```
public static Image createImage(int width, int height)
```

Typically you would create a mutable Image for off-screen drawing, perhaps for an animation or to reduce flicker if the device's display is not double buffered.

Any Image you pass to Alert, ChoiceGroup, ImageItem, or List should be immutable. To create an immutable Image from a mutable one, use the following method: public static Image createImage(Image image).

Editing a List

List provides methods for adding items, removing elements, and examining elements. Each element in the List has an index. The first element is at index 0, then next at index 1, and so forth. You can replace an element with setElement() or add an element to the end of the list with appendElement(). The insertElement() method adds a new element to the list at the given index; this bumps all elements at that position and higher up by one.

```
public void setElement(int index, String stringElement, Image imageElement)
public void insertElement(int index, String stringElement, Image imageElement)
public int appendElement(String stringElement, Image imageElement)
```

You can examine the string or image for a given element by supplying its index. Similarly, you can use deleteElement() to remove an element from the List.

```
public String getString(int index)
public Image getImage(int index)
public void deleteElement(int index)
```

Finally, the `size()` method returns the number of elements in the List.

```
public int size()
```

Working with List Selections

You can find out whether a particular element in a List is selected by supplying the element's index to the following method:

```
public boolean isSelected(int index)
```

For EXCLUSIVE and IMPLICIT lists, the index of the single selected element is returned from the following method:

```
public int getSelectedIndex()
```

If you call getSelectedIndex() on a MULTIPLE list, it will return –1.
To change the current selection programmatically, use setSelectedIndex().

```
public void setSelectedIndex(int index, boolean selected)
```

Finally, List allows you to set or get the selection state *en masse* with the following methods. The supplied arrays must have as many array elements as there are list elements.

```
public int getSelectedFlags(boolean[] selectedArray_return)
public void setSelectedFlags(boolean[] selectedArray)
```

An Example

The example in Listing 6-1 shows a simple MIDlet that could be part of a travel reservation application. The user chooses what type of reservation to make. This example uses an IMPLICIT list, which is essentially a menu.

Listing 6-1. The TravelList source code.

```
import java.io.*;
import javax.microedition.midlet.*;
import javax.microedition.lcdui.*;
```

```java
public class TravelList extends MIDlet {
  public void startApp() {
    final String[] stringElements = { "Airplane", "Car", "Hotel" };
    Image[] imageElements = { loadImage("/airplane.png"),
        loadImage("/car.png"), loadImage("/hotel.png") };
    final List list = new List("Reservation type", List.IMPLICIT,
        stringElements, imageElements);

    final Command nextCommand = new Command("Next", Command.SCREEN, 0);
    Command quitCommand = new Command("Quit", Command.SCREEN, 0);
    list.addCommand(nextCommand);
    list.addCommand(quitCommand);
    list.setCommandListener(new CommandListener() {
      public void commandAction(Command c, Displayable s) {
        if (c == nextCommand || c == List.SELECT_COMMAND) {
          int index = list.getSelectedIndex();
          System.out.println("Your selection: " + stringElements[index]);
          // Move on to the next screen. Here, we just exit.
          notifyDestroyed();
        }
        else notifyDestroyed();
      }
    });

    Display.getDisplay(this).setCurrent(list);
  }

  public void pauseApp() {}

  public void destroyApp(boolean unconditional) {}

  private Image loadImage(String name) {
    Image image = null;
    try {
      image = Image.createImage(name);
    }
    catch (IOException ioe) {
      System.out.println(ioe);
    }

    return image;
  }
}
```

To see images in this example, you'll need to either download the examples from the book's Web site or supply your own images. With the J2MEWTK, image files should go in the *res* directory of your J2MEWTK project directory. TravelList expects to find three images named *airplane.png, car.png,* and *hotel.png.*

Construction of the List itself is very straightforward. Our application also includes a **Next** command and a **Quit** command, which are both added to the List. An inner class is registered as the CommandListener for the List. If the **Next** command or the List's IMPLICIT command are fired off, we simply retrieve the selected item from the List and print it to the console.

The **Next** command, in fact, is not strictly necessary in this example since you can achieve the same result by clicking the select button on one of the elements in the List. Nevertheless, it might be a good idea to leave it there. Maybe all of the other screens in your application have a **Next** command, so you could keep it for user interface consistency. It never hurts to provide the user with more than one way of doing things, either.

The difference between EXCLUSIVE and IMPLICIT lists can be subtle. Try changing the List in this example to EXCLUSIVE to see how the user experience is different.

Creating Advanced Interfaces with Forms

A Form is a screen that can include an arbitrary collection of user-interface controls, called items. In a movie ticket reservation MIDlet, you might use a form to allow the user to enter a date and a Zip code on one screen.

Keep in mind that the minimum screen size for a MID is 96×54 pixels. You can't fit a whole lot on a screen this size, nor should you try to. Forms that don't fit on the screen will automatically scroll as needed, so your MIDlet will be able to show forms, regardless of the screen size. Scrolling forms tend to be confusing to users, however, so you should keep your forms as small as possible.

The javax.microedition.ldcui.Form class itself is fairly simple. One way to create a Form is by specifying a title:

```
public Form(String title)
```

In essence, a Form is a collection of items. Each item is represented by an instance of the Item class. If you have all the items ahead of time, you can pass them to Form's other constructor:

```
public Form(String title, Item[] items)
```

As a subclass of Screen, Form inherits both a title and a ticker. Given the small screen size of a MID, however, you may want to avoid using a ticker with your forms.

Form's grandparent class, Displayable, gives Form the capabilities of displaying commands and firing command events. Again, you should probably keep commands simple with forms; in many cases a **Next** and a **Back** will probably be sufficient.

Managing Items

Items may be added and removed, even while the Form is showing. The order of items is important, as well; most MIDP implementations will display a form's items top to bottom, scrolling the form as needed if there are more items than available screen space.

To add an Item to the bottom of a form, use one of the append() methods. The first one can be used to add any Item implementation. The second two append() methods are strictly for convenience; behind the scenes, a StringItem or an ImageItem will be created for you.

```
public int append(Item item)
public int append(String str)
public int append(Image image)
```

Every item in a form has an index. You can place an item at a specific index (replacing the previous item at that index) using the method:

```
public void set(int index, Item item)
```

Alternately, if you'd like to add an item somewhere in the middle of the form, just supply the desired index for the new item to the insert() method. Subsequent items will move up by one index.

```
public void insert(int index, Item item)
```

To remove an item from a form, use delete().

```
public void delete(int index)
```

If you forget what you put in a form, you can find out the number of items and retrieve them with the following methods:

```
public int size()
public Item get(int index)
```

The Item Pantry

The MIDP specification includes a handy toolbox of items that can be used to build forms. I'll cover each of them briefly in this section and show how some of them look in Sun's MIDP reference implementation.

The Item Class

All of the items that can be added to forms descend from the `javax.microedition.lcdui.Item` class. `Item` doesn't specify much, just a `getLabel()` and `setLabel()` method. All `Item`s have a string label, although it may or may not be shown by the specific subclass.

StringItem

`StringItem` represents a simple text label. Although it has both a label and a value, the two are indistinguishable in Sun's J2MEWTK implementation. For example, consider the following code:

```
Form form = new Form("FormTitle");
StringItem stringItem = new StringItem("Label", "Value");
form.append(stringItem);
```

The form produced by this code (plus a **Back** command) is shown in Figure 6-3.

*Figure 6-3. A form with a single `StringItem` and a **Back** command*

You can use `null` for the `StringItem`'s label or value to indicate that it should not be shown on the screen. `StringItem` inherits `setLabel()` and `getLabel()` methods from `Item`. It also includes `getText()` and `setText()` methods for accessing and adjusting the string value.

TextField

`TextField` represents an editable string. Figure 6-4 shows a `TextField` with a label of **TextFieldTitle** and a value of **text**.

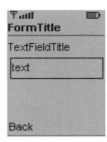

Figure 6-4. A form with a single TextField *and a* **Back** *command*

When the user selects the TextField, an editing screen is shown (although it's up to the implementation to decide exactly how to allow editing). The editing screen in Sun's J2MEWTK emulator is just a TextBox, as shown in Figure 6-5. Choosing the **Save** command returns the user to the form with the new text. Choosing **Back** returns the user to the form, canceling changes.

Figure 6-5. Editing a TextField

TextFields can limit input. The following constants are defined:

- ANY allows any type of input.

- NUMERIC restricts the input to numbers.

- PHONENUMBER requires a telephone number.

- EMAILADDR input must be an e-mail address.

- URL input must be a URL.

- PASSWORD entered characters are not shown, generally represented by asterisks.

These input types might look familiar; they're the same ones used by TextBox, which I covered in the previous chapter. As with TextBox, PASSWORD can be combined with other types using the OR operator.

To create a TextField, you need to supply the label, text value, maximum length, and input constraints.

```
public TextField(String label, String text, int maxSize, int constraints)
```

For an initially empty TextField, pass null for the text parameter.

ImageItem

Forms can also contain images, which are represented by instances of ImageItem. ImageItems have several pieces of associated data:

- A *label* may be displayed with the image.

- The *layout* determines the placement of the image.

- *Alternate text* is displayed if the image cannot be shown.

To create an ImageItem, just supply the Image that is to be displayed, the label, layout, and alternate text.

ImageItem defines constants for the layout parameter. The simplest thing is to specify the default value, LAYOUT_DEFAULT. If you need more control, combine a horizontal value with a vertical value. The horizontal values are LAYOUT_LEFT, LAYOUT_CENTER, and LAYOUT_RIGHT. The vertical values are LAYOUT_NEWLINE_BEFORE and LAYOUT_NEWLINE_AFTER.

Figure 6-6. An ImageItem *shown in 4-bit grayscale*

DateField

DateField is an extremely handy mechanism by which users can enter dates, times, or both. It's up to the implementation to determine some reasonable way for users to enter dates and times; you, as the MIDlet programmer, can simply use DateField and not worry about the implementation.

To create a DateField, specify a label and a type. Three constants in the DateField class describe the different types:

- DATE displays an editable date.

- TIME displays an editable time.

- DATE_TIME displays both a date and a time.

DateField provides two constructors. The first uses the default time zone, while the second allows you to specify a TimeZone explicitly:

```
public DateField(String label, int mode)
public DateField(String label, int mode, TimeZone timeZone)
```

In essence, a DateField is an editor for a java.util.Date. As you saw in Chapter 4, Dates represent points in time. DateField takes the role of translating between a Date and strings that humans can read, much like the Calendar class. You can set or get the Date represented by the DateField using the following methods:

```
public Date getDate()
public void setDate(Date date)
```

In the J2MEWTK emulator, a DateField appears as shown in Figure 6-7a. Note that if you do not initialize the Date before showing the DateField, it will appear unitialized, as shown in Figure 6-7b.

When the user selects either the date or time portion of the DateField and selects it for editing, the MIDP implementation provides some kind of appropriate editor. Sun's reference implementation provides the editors shown in Figure 6-7c and Figure 6-7d.

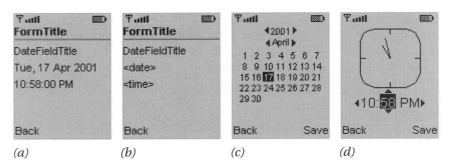

(a)   *(b)*   *(c)*   *(d)*

Figure 6-7. DateField *in Sun's J2MEWTK emulator*

Gauge

A Gauge represents an integer value. It's up to the implementation to decide how to display itself. In Sun's MIDP implementation, a Gauge appears as shown in Figure 6-8.

Figure 6-8. A Gauge

The value of the Gauge can be retrieved and modified with the getValue() and setValue() methods. This value runs from 0 to a variable maximum value. The maximum for the Gauge can be retrieved and modified with the getMaxValue() and setMaxValue() methods.

The visual appearance of the Gauge is an approximation of the Gauge's value. The Gauge shown in Figure 6-8 could, for example, have a value of 7 and a maximum of 10, or perhaps a value of 42 and a maximum of 61.

In an *interactive* Gauge, the user can modify the value. Again, it's up to the implementation to decide exactly how this works. In Sun's reference implementation, the left and right navigation buttons can be used to modify a Gauge's value.

Now that you understand everything about Gauges, you'll understand the constructor:

```
public Gauge(String label, boolean interactive,
    int maxValue, int initialValue)
```

For example, the following code creates an interactive Gauge with a maximum value of 24 and an initial value of 2:

```
Gauge g = new Gauge("Power", true, 24, 2);
```

ChoiceGroup

The final class in the Form arsenal of Items is ChoiceGroup. ChoiceGroup offers a list of choices. It is very similar to javax.microedition.lcdui.List, which was described at the beginning of this chapter. This similarity is more than coincidental; `ChoiceGroup` and `List` both implement the `Choice` interface, which is the wellspring of all of the instance methods in both classes.

If you read the section about `List`, you already know almost everything you need to know to use `ChoiceGroup`, because the instance methods work exactly the same way.

`ChoiceGroup` features the following constructors:

```
public ChoiceGroup(String label, int choiceType)
public ChoiceGroup(String label, int choiceType, String[] stringElements,
    Image[] imageElements)
```

The `choiceType` should look familiar; it can be either `EXCLUSIVE`, `MULTIPLE`, or `IMPLICIT`, the constants defined in the `Choice` interface. In fact, `ChoiceGroup`'s constructors work exactly like `List`'s constructors. The `ChoiceGroup` appears like any other element in the `Form`; Figure 6-9 shows an example.

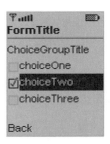

Figure 6-9. A `MULTIPLE` `ChoiceGroup` *in a* `Form`

Understanding Form Layout

Forms are mostly vertical beasts. In general, items added to a form will appear in a vertical stack. If the items don't all fit on the screen, the form allows the user to scroll as needed.

The exceptions to this rule are `StringItems` and `ImageItems`. These items may be laid out left-to-right if there is enough space on the screen. However, it's up to the implementation to decide exactly how a form is laid out. In the J2MEWTK 1.0.1 emulator, `StringItems` and `ImageItems` are always stacked vertically.

Responding to Item Changes

Most items in a Form fire events when the user changes them. Your application can listen for these events by registering an ItemStateListener with the Form using the following method:

```
public void setItemStateListener(ItemStateListener iListener)
```

ItemStateListener is an interface with a single method. This method is called every time an item in a Form is changed:

```
public void itemStateChanged(Item item)
```

The following example creates a Form with two items, an interactive Gauge and a StringItem. As you adjust the Gauge, its value is reflected in the StringItem using the ItemStateListener mechanism.

```
import javax.microedition.midlet.*;
import javax.microedition.lcdui.*;

public class GaugeTracker
    extends MIDlet
    implements ItemStateListener {
  private Gauge mGauge;
  private StringItem mStringItem;

  public GaugeTracker() {
    int initialValue = 5;
    mGauge = new Gauge("GaugeTitle", true, 10, initialValue);
    mStringItem = new StringItem(null, "[value]");
    itemStateChanged(mGauge);
  }

  public void itemStateChanged(Item item) {
    if (item == mGauge)
      mStringItem.setText("Value = " + mGauge.getValue());
  }
```

```
  public void startApp() {
    Form form = new Form("GaugeTracker");
    // Now add the selected items.
    form.append(mGauge);
    form.append(mStringItem);
    form.setItemStateListener(this);

Display.getDisplay(this).setCurrent(form);
  }

public void pauseApp() {}

  public void destroyApp(boolean unconditional) {}
}
```

Summary

This chapter described MIDP's advanced user-interface screens, List and Form. A List is a list of elements that allows for single or multiple selections. You supply the items—it's up to the implementation to figure out how to show them, how the user navigates through them, and how the user selects items. Forms are generalized screens that are built up from a collection of Items. The MIDP API supplies a handy toolbox of Items—everything from simple string and image Items to the more complex DateField and ChoiceGroup.

Even though List and Form are very capable, you should use them sparingly, particularly Form. Small devices have small screens, so you don't want to put much information in each screen, especially if it's going to force the user to scroll up and down a lot. Furthermore, ease of use is crucial on consumer devices like mobile phones and pagers. Make sure your interface is clean, intuitive, and as simple as it can possibly be.

CHAPTER 7

Persistent Storage

MIDP applications have to run seamlessly on many devices. You've already seen how this can be a challenge in the user-interface arena. The trick there was to use abstract concepts that would be mapped to the screen by a device-specific implementation.

MIDP's approach to persistent storage is basically the same. Your application could run on a MID with flash ROM, battery-backed RAM, or even a small hard disk. MIDP applications don't really care; all they know about are small databases called record stores. It's up to the device's MIDP implementation to map record stores in some reasonable manner to whatever persistent storage is available.

These are *small* amounts of data we're talking about; the MIDP specification dictates that the minimum amount of persistent storage is only 8KB.

Overview

Persistent storage in MIDP is centered around record stores. A *record store* is a small database that contains pieces of data called *records*. Record stores are represented by instances of `javax.microedition.rms.RecordStore`. The scope of a record store is limited to a single MIDlet suite. Said another way, a MIDlet can only access record stores that were created by a MIDlet in the same suite. Figure 7-1 shows the relationship between MIDlet suites and record stores.

Record stores are identified by a name. Within a MIDlet suite's record stores, the names must be unique.

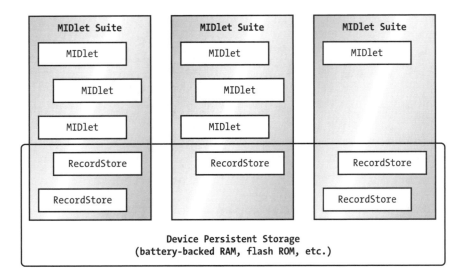

Figure 7-1. RecordStore*s belong to MIDlet suites.*

Managing RecordStores

The RecordStore class serves two purposes. First, it defines an API for manipulating individual records. Second, it defines an API (mostly static methods) for managing record stores.

Opening, Closing, and Removing Record Stores

To open a record store, you simply need to name it.

```
public static RecordStore openRecordStore(String recordStoreName,
    boolean createIfNecessary) throws RecordStoreException,
    RecordStoreFullException, RecordStoreNotFoundException
```

If the record store does not exist, the createIfNecessary parameter determines whether a new record store will be created or not. If the record store does not exist, and the createIfNecessary parameter is false, then a RecordStoreNotFoundException will be thrown.

The following code opens a record store named "Address."

```
RecordStore rs = RecordStore.openRecordStore("Address", true);
```

The record store will be created if it does not already exist.

An open record store can be closed by calling the `closeRecordStore()` method. As with anything that can be opened and closed, it's a good idea to close record stores when you're finished with them. Memory and processing power are in short supply on a small device, so you should remember to clean up after yourself as much as possible. You probably shouldn't even keep a record store open over the lifetime of the MIDlet; after all, your MIDlet may be paused by the device's application manager, and it would be unwise to have open resources while the MIDlet is Paused.

To find out all the record stores available to a particular MIDlet suite, call the `listRecordStores()` method:

```
public static String[] listRecordStores()
```

Finally, to remove a record store, call the static `deleteRecordStore()` method. The record store and its contained records will be deleted.

Record Store Size

Record stores consist of records; each record is simply an array of bytes. On space-constrained devices, you'll probably want to keep a close eye on the size of your record stores. To find out the number of bytes used by a record store, call the following method on a `RecordStore` instance:

```
public int getSize()
```

You can find out how much more space is available by calling the following method:

```
public int getSizeAvailable()
```

Note that this method returns the total space available in the record store, which is not the same as the amount of record data that is available. That is, there is some overhead associated with each record in the record store; the `getSizeAvailable()` method returns the amount of space available for both record data and overhead.

Version and Timestamp

Record stores maintain both a version number and a timestamp. The version number is updated every time the record store is modified. It is represented by an integer and can be retrieved by calling `getVersion()`.

The record store also remembers the last time it was modified. This moment in time is represented by a `long`, which can be retrieved with `getLastModified()`.

The long represents the number of milliseconds since midnight on January 1, 1970. You may recall (from Chapter 4) that this is the same way that Date uses a long to represent a moment in time. If you need to examine the timestamp of a record store, you can create a Date from the long timestamp. Then you could use a Calendar to translate from a Date to calendar fields like month, day, hour, and minute.

Working with Records

A *record* is simply an array of bytes. Each record in a RecordStore is has an integer identification number. Figure 7-2 shows a diagram of a RecordStore with four records.

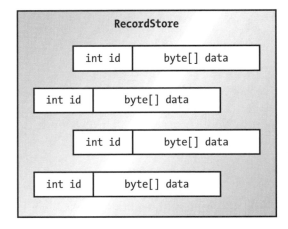

Figure 7-2. Inside a RecordStore

Adding Records

To add a new record, supply the byte array to the addRecord() method:

```
public int addRecord(byte[] data, int offset, int numBytes)
    throws RecordStoreNotOpenException,
        RecordStoreException,
        RecordStoreFullException
```

The added record will be numBytes long, taken from the data array starting at offset. The new record's ID is returned. Most other record operations need this ID to identify a particular record.

The following code fragment illustrates adding a new record to a record store named rs. It creates a byte array from a String, and then writes the entire byte array into a new record.

```
String record = "This is a record";
byte[] data = record.getBytes();
int id = rs.addRecord(data, 0, data.length);
```

Retrieving Records

You can retrieve a record by supplying the record ID to the following method:

```
public byte[] getRecord(int recordId)
    throws RecordStoreNotOpenException,
           InvalidRecordIDException,
           RecordStoreException
```

This method returns a freshly created byte array containing the record with the requested ID. An alternate version of this method puts the record data into an array that you supply:

```
public int getRecord(int recordId, byte[] buffer, int offset)
throws RecordStoreNotOpenException,
           InvalidRecordIDException,
           RecordStoreException
```

This method returns the number of bytes that were copied into your array. If the array you supply is not large enough to hold the record, an ArrayOutOfBoundsException will be thrown. You can find out the size of a particular record ahead of time by calling getRecordSize().

Given a RecordStore rs and a record ID id, here is one way to retrieve a record's data:

```
byte[] retrieved = new byte[rs.getRecordSize(id)];
rs.getRecord(id, retrieved, 0);
String retrievedString = new String(retrieved);
```

If you're going to be pulling many records out of the record store, you probably won't want to create a new byte array each time. For efficiency, you would create one array and use it over and over again to pull records out of the record store. One way to create the buffer is to make it as large as the largest record in the record store. If that's not practical, or if you don't know how large the largest record will be, you can simply check the size of each record before you retrieve it. If you come across a record that's larger than the buffer, you could create a larger buffer.

If you're not worried about memory usage or speed, then you might as well use the other form of getRecord(), which is essentially the same as the previous code example:

```
byte[] retrieved = rs.getRecord(id);
```

Deleting and Replacing Records

So far you've seen how to add new records and retrieve them. There are two more record operations supported by RecordStore. First, you can remove a record by passing its ID to deleteRecord(). Second, you can replace the data of an existing record by calling the following method:

```
public void setRecord(int recordId, byte[] newData, int offset, int numBytes)
    throws RecordStoreNotOpenException,
           InvalidRecordIDException,
           RecordStoreException,
           RecordStoreFullException
```

Getting RecordStore Record Information

The RecordStore keeps an internal counter that it uses to assign record IDs. You can find out what the next record ID will be by calling getNextRecordID(). And you can find out how many records exist in the RecordStore by calling getNumRecords().

Saving User Preferences

Let's put some of this knowledge to work. This section details a simple MIDlet that saves a user name and password in a RecordStore. Each time the MIDlet is used, it can load the user name and password from the RecordStore instead of requiring the user to enter the same information over and over.

The MIDlet itself is very simple. Its only screen is a Form that contains fields for entering the user name and password. It uses a helper class, Preferences, to do all the RecordStore work. Listing 7-1 shows the source code for the MIDlet.

Listing 7-1. Source code for RecordMIDlet.

```java
import javax.microedition.midlet.*;
import javax.microedition.lcdui.*;

public class RecordMIDlet extends MIDlet {
  private Preferences mPreferences;
  private Form mForm;
  private TextField mUserField, mPasswordField;

  public void startApp() {
    // Try to load the user and password from a recordstore.
    mPreferences = Preferences.getInstance();

    if (mForm == null) {
      mForm = new Form("Login");
      mUserField = new TextField("Name",
          mPreferences.getUser(), 32, 0);
      mPasswordField = new TextField("Password",
          mPreferences.getPassword(), 32, 0);
      mForm.append(mUserField);
      mForm.append(mPasswordField);

      mForm.addCommand(new Command("Exit", Command.EXIT, 0));
      mForm.setCommandListener(new CommandListener() {
        public void commandAction(Command c, Displayable s) {
          if (c.getCommandType() == Command.EXIT) {
            destroyApp(true);
            notifyDestroyed();
          }
        }
      });
    }

    Display.getDisplay(this).setCurrent(mForm);
  }

  public void pauseApp() {}

  public void destroyApp(boolean unconditional) {
    // Save the user name and password.
    mPreferences.setUser(mUserField.getString());
    mPreferences.setPassword(mPasswordField.getString());
    mPreferences.store();
  }
}
```

All the RecordStore work is encapsulated in the Preferences class, shown in Listing 7-2. Preferences is a wrapper for a user name and password, stored as String member variables mUser and mPassword. A static method, getInstance(), provides access to a single Preferences object. Each time getInstance() is called, the user name and password are loaded from a RecordStore.

Listing 7-2. Preferences is a helper class that encapsulates RecordStore access.

```
import javax.microedition.rms.*;

public class Preferences {
  private static Preferences sInstance;

  public static Preferences getInstance() {
    if (sInstance == null)
      sInstance = new Preferences("", "");

    RecordStore rs = null;
    try {
      rs = RecordStore.openRecordStore("Preferences", true);
    }
    catch (RecordStoreException rse) {
      return null;
    }

    String user, password;
    user = password = "";
    try {
      byte[] userBytes = rs.getRecord(1);
      byte[] passwordBytes = rs.getRecord(2);
      user = new String(userBytes);
      password = new String(passwordBytes);
    }
    catch (RecordStoreException rse) {}
    catch (NullPointerException npe) {}
    try { rs.closeRecordStore(); }
    catch (RecordStoreException rse) {}

    sInstance.setUser(user);
    sInstance.setPassword(password);

    return sInstance;
  }
```

```
    private String mUser, mPassword;

  private Preferences(String user, String password) {
    setUser(user);
    setPassword(password);
  }

  public String getUser() { return mUser; }
  public String getPassword() { return mPassword; }

  public void setUser(String user) { mUser = user; }
  public void setPassword(String password) { mPassword = password; }

  public void store() {
    RecordStore rs = null;
    try {
      rs = RecordStore.openRecordStore("Preferences", false);
    }
    catch (RecordStoreException rse) { return; }

    try {
      byte[] userBytes = mUser.getBytes();
      byte[] passwordBytes = mPassword.getBytes();
      int n = rs.getNumRecords();
      if (n == 0) {
        rs.addRecord(userBytes, 0, userBytes.length);
        rs.addRecord(passwordBytes, 0, passwordBytes.length);
      }
      else {
        rs.setRecord(1, userBytes, 0, userBytes.length);
        rs.setRecord(2, passwordBytes, 0, passwordBytes.length);
      }
    }
    catch (RecordStoreException rse) {}

    try { rs.closeRecordStore(); }
    catch (RecordStoreException rse) {}
  }
}
```

RecordMIDlet saves the updated values back to the RecordStore in its destroyApp() method. It saves the user name and password from the user interface in the Preferences object, then calls the store() method to write the new values out to the RecordStore. The store() method simply adds the records if the RecordStore is empty, or sets the existing records to the new values.

To test out the MIDlet, enter some text into the user name and password fields. Then exit the MIDlet and restart it. You will see the same values loaded into the text fields.

Listening for Record Changes

RecordStores support a JavaBeans-style listener mechanism. Interested objects can listen for changes to a record store by registering themselves as listeners.

The listener interface is javax.microedition.rms.RecordListener. You can manage a RecordStore's listeners with the following two methods:

```
public void addRecordListener(RecordListener listener)
public void removeRecordListener(RecordListener listener)
```

The RecordListener interface has three methods: recordAdded(), recordChanged(), and recordDeleted(). These are called whenever a record is added, changed, or deleted. Each method is passed the RecordStore involved and the ID of the record in question.

Performing RecordStore Queries

The real power of a database is being able to pull out just the record or records you want. In a larger database, this is called *performing a query*. In the RecordStore world, you use the enumerateRecords() method:

```
public RecordEnumeration enumerateRecords(RecordFilter filter,
    RecordComparator comparator, boolean keepUpdated)
    throws RecordStoreNotOpenException
```

This single method in RecordStore involves three different interfaces that you've never seen before. Let's start with the big picture first, and then drill down into the new interfaces.

The enumerateRecords() method returns a sorted subset of the records in a RecordStore. The RecordFilter determines which records will be included in the subset, while the RecordComparator is used to sort them. The returned RecordEnumeration allows you to navigate through the returned records.

RecordFilter

The simplest interface is RecordFilter. When you call enumerateRecords() on a
RecordStore, each record's data is retrieved. RecordFilter has a single method,
matches(), which is called for each record. A record filter should examine the
record data and return true if the record should be included in the results
returned from enumerateRecords().

Here's a simple RecordFilter implementation that will only select records
whose first byte of data is 7:

```
public class SevenFilter
    implements javax.microedition.rms.RecordFilter {
  public boolean matches(byte[] candidate) {
    if (candidate.length == 0) return false;
    return (candidate[0] == 7);
  }
}
```

RecordComparator

The job of a RecordComparator implementation is to determine the order of two
sets of record data. RecordComparator is similar to the java.util.Comparator
interface in J2SE.

To implement the RecordComparator interface, you just need to define one
method:

```
public int compare(byte[] rec1, byte[] rec2)
```

This method examines the data contained in rec1 and rec2 and determines
which of them should come first in a sorted list. It should return one of the following constants defined in RecordComparator:

- PRECEDES indicates that rec1 should come before rec2.

- FOLLOWS indicates that rec1 should come after rec2.

- EQUIVALENT signals that rec1 and rec2 are the same, at least as far as sorting
  is concerned.

The following simple implementation compares each byte of the given
records and sorts them numerically. If the two records have the same data, up to
the length of the shorter one, then they are deemed EQUIVALENT.

```
public class SimpleComparator
    implements javax.microedition.rms.RecordComparator {
  public int compare(byte[] rec1, byte[] rec2) {
    int limit = Math.min(rec1.length, rec2.length);

    for (int index = 0; index < limit; index++) {
      if (rec1[index] < rec2[index])
        return PRECEDES;
      else if (rec1[index] > rec2[index])
        return FOLLOWS;
    }
    return EQUIVALENT;
  }
}
```

Working with RecordEnumeration

RecordStore's enumerateRecords() method returns an implementation of the RecordEnumeration interface. RecordEnumeration is surprisingly complicated. Its basic function is to allow you to iterate through the records retrieved from the RecordStore. Unlike a regular J2SE Enumeration or Iterator, however, RecordEnumeration allows you to scroll through its contents both forward and backward. In addition, you can peek at the next or previous record ID. Finally, RecordEnumeration offers the possibility of keeping its data synchronized with the actual RecordStore. Behind the scenes, this is accomplished by registering the RecordEnumeration as a listener for RecordStore changes.

The basic operation of RecordEnumeration is to iterate through a set of records. You can find out if there's a next record by calling hasNextElement(). If the next record exists, you can retrieve its data by calling the following method:

```
public byte[] nextRecord()
    throws InvalidRecordIDException,
           RecordStoreNotOpenException,
           RecordStoreException
```

Alternately, you can retrieve the next record's ID by calling this method:

```
public int nextRecordId() throws InvalidRecordIDException
```

You can't really have your cake and eat it, though; both nextRecord() and nextRecordId() advance the RecordEnumeration to the next record. If you want to retrieve both the ID and the data for the next record, you'd need to call nextRecordId() and then retrieve the record data directly from the RecordStore.

A typical use of RecordEnumeration would be to walk straight through the selected records, like this:

```
// Open a RecordStore rs
// Create a RecordFilter rf
// Create a RecordComparator rc

RecordEnumeration re = rs.enumerateRecords(rf, rc, false);
while (re.hasNextElement()) {
  byte[] recordBytes = re.nextRecord();
  // Process the retrieved bytes.
}
```

As you're moving through the selected records, you can also move backward. RecordEnumeration includes hasPreviousElement(), previousRecord(), and previousRecordId() methods that work just their next counterparts.

Four out of the five ways to move the current position in the RecordEnumeration are the nextRecord(), nextRecordId(), previousRecord(), or previousRecordId() methods. The fifth method is kind of like a rewind button: reset() moves the record pointer back to the very beginning of the selected records.

When you're finished using a RecordEnumeration, you should release its resources. You can do this by calling destroy(), after which the RecordEnumeration is no longer usable.

Keeping a RecordEnumeration Up to Date

In a multithreaded environment, it's entirely possible that a RecordStore will change at the same time you're iterating through a RecordEnumeration for the same RecordStore. There are two ways to deal with this.

The first thing you can do is call rebuild(), which explicitly rebuilds the RecordEnumeration based on the RecordFilter and RecordComparator you originally specified.

The other possibility is to request a RecordEnumeration that is automatically updated with any changes to the underlying RecordStore. You can do this by passing true for the keepUpdated parameter of RecordStore's enumerateRecords() method. You can find out if the RecordEnumeration is automatically updated by calling isKeptUpdated(). Furthermore, you can change its state by calling keepUpdated().

Automatically updated RecordEnumerations register themselves as RecordListeners with the underlying RecordStore. Each time the RecordStore is changed, the RecordEnumeration is rebuilt. Keep in mind that this is an expensive operation (in terms of time), so if there are many RecordStore changes, you'll be paying a price for it.

Using Resource Files

Another form of persistent storage is resource files. Accessing resource files is very simple, but they are important nevertheless. Resource files can be images, text, or other types of files that are stored in a MIDlet suite JAR.

You can access a resource file as an InputStream by using the getResourceAsStream() method in Class. A typical usage looks like this:

```
InputStream in = this.getClass().getResourceAsStream("/Robotag-t.png");
```

Summary

The MIDP API for persistent storage is deliberately abstract in recognition that small devices will likely have many different methods for storing data. In MIDP, the central concept for persistent storage is the record store, which is a collection of bits of data called records. A record store is really a tiny database, but the details of exactly how it is stored are left to the device implementation. The javax.microedition.rms.RecordStore class encapsulates all access to persistent storage. It provides methods for accessing and manipulating RecordStores, as well as methods for working with individual records. For more advanced RecordStore work, methods and interfaces exist to help keep track of changes to a RecordStore or to perform RecordStore queries.

CHAPTER 8

Connecting to the World

It's cool running Java on mobile phones and pagers, but the real kicker is getting your MIDlets connected to the Internet. With an Internet connection, you can write applications that allow you to access information and do work from your mobile telephone, from wherever you are in the world.

The Generic Connection Framework

The CLDC defines an extremely flexible API for network connections, the *generic connection framework*. It's all contained in the `javax.microedition.io` package and based around the `Connection` interface. Figure 8-1 details the `Connection` interface and its various child interfaces. I've omitted the methods of `DatagramConnection` and `HttpConnection` in this diagram; we'll explore them in detail later.

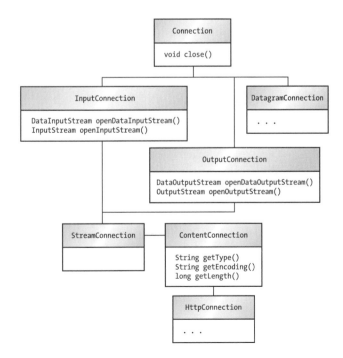

Figure 8-1. The Connection *family tree*

The link between the Connection interfaces and reality is a class called javax.microedition.io.Connector. In fact, it's the only class in the javax.microedition.io package. The basic idea is that you pass a connection string to one of Connector's static methods and get back some Connection implementation. *A connection string* looks something like a URL, but there are various other possibilities. The connection string socket://apress.com:79 might open a TCP/IP connection to apress.com on port 79, then return a StreamConnection implementation.

MIDP simplifies this generic framework considerably by only requiring one type of connection, Hypertext Transfer Protocol (HTTP). You pass an HTTP URL to Connector and get back an implementation of HttpConnection. Although MIDP compliant devices may support additional types of connections, HTTP is the only one you should depend on.

HttpConnection's methods are detailed in Figure 8-2. Most of the methods in HttpConnection have to do with details of HTTP, which I won't cover here. I'll cover everything you need to know to connect to a server here, including both GET and POST requests. If you need to dig deeper, you can read RFC 2616 (one of the Internet standards documents), available at http://www.faqs.org/rfcs/rfc2616.html. Note that MIDP uses a subset of the full HTTP 1.1; only the GET, POST, and HEAD commands are required.

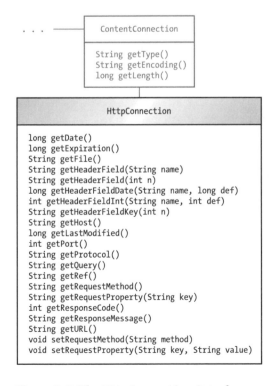

Figure 8-2. The HttpConnection *interface*

Review of HTTP

This section presents a brief review of the Hypertext Transfer Protocol. The whole story is in RFC 2616; this section covers the essentials.

Requests and Responses

HTTP is built around requests and responses. A client sends a request for a server—something like, "Please give me such-and-so HTML page." The server sends back a response—something like, "Here's the file," or "I don't know what you're talking about."

Requests and responses have two parts: headers and content. If you type a URL into your browser, the browser creates an HTTP request (mostly headers) and sends it to a server. The server finds the requested file and sends it back in an HTTP response. The response headers describe things like the type of Web server, the file type of the response, the length of the response, and other information. The response content is the data of the file itself.

Parameters

Browsers and other HTTP clients request specific named resources from HTTP servers. In addition, clients can pass parameters to the server. Parameters are simple name and value pairs. For example, a client might send a "userid" parameter with a value of "jonathan" to a server.

When a browser is the HTTP client, parameters are generally collected from HTML forms. You've seen these forms, like the one where you fill in your shipping address and your credit card number. Form values are sent as parameters to a Web server when you click the **Submit** or **Next** button on the form.

The client encodes parameters before they are sent to the server. Parameters are passed as name and value pairs; multiple parameters are separated by ampersands. The exact way that parameters are encoded is documented in the J2SE documentation for `java.net.URLEncoder`. The rules are relatively simple.

- The space character is converted to a plus (+) sign.

- The following characters remain unchanged: lowercase letters a through z, uppercase letters A through Z, the numbers 0 through 9, the period (.), the hyphen (-), the asterisk (*), and the underscore (_).

- All other characters are converted into '%xy,' where 'xy' is a hexadecimal number that represents the low eight bits of the character.

GET, HEAD, and POST

The simplest HTTP operation is GET. This is what happens when you type a URL into your browser. The browser says, "GET me this URL," and the server responds with the headers and content of the response.

With a GET request, parameters are added to the end of the URL in encoded form. For example, suppose the following URL maps to a servlet or some other server-side component of your application:

```
http://jonathanknudsen.com/simple
```

Adding a parameter is easy. If you want to pass a parameter with a name of "user" and a value of "jonathan," you would use the following URL:

```
http://jonathanknudsen.com/simple?user=jonathan
```

Additional name and value pairs can be added, separated by ampersands:

```
http://jonathanknudsen.com/simple?user=jonathan&zip=08540&day=saturday
```

The HEAD operation is identical to GET, but the server sends back only the headers of the response.

POST is basically the same as GET, but parameters are handled differently. Instead of being pasted on the end of the URL, as they are with GET, the parameters are passed as the body of the request. They are encoded in the same way.

Making a Connection with HTTP GET

Loading data from a server is startlingly simple, particularly if you're performing an HTTP GET. Simply pass a URL to Connector's static open() method. The returned Connection will probably be an implementation of HttpConnection, but you can just treat it as an InputConnection. Then get the corresponding and read data to your heart's content.

In code, it looks something like this:

```
String url = "http://jonathanknudsen.com/simple";
InputConnection ic = (InputConnection)Connector.open(url);
InputStream in = ic.openInputStream();
// Read stuff from the InputStream
ic.close();
```

Most of the methods involved can throw a java.io.IOException. I've omitted the try and catch blocks from the example for clarity.

That's all there is to it. You can now connect your MIDlets to the world.

Passing Parameters

With HTTP GET, all parameters are passed to the server in the body of the URL. This makes it easy to send parameters to the server. The following code fragment shows how two parameters can be passed:

```
String url = "http://localhost/midp/simple?pOne=one+bit&pTwo=two";
InputConnection ic = (InputConnection)Connector.open(url);
InputStream in = ic.openInputStream();
```

The first parameter is named "pOne" and has "one bit," as a value; the second parameter is named "pTwo" and has "two" as a value.

A Simple Example

HTTP isn't all about exchanging HTML pages. It's actually a generic file-exchange protocol. In this section, we'll look at an example that loads an image from the network and displays it. Listing 8-1 shows the source code for ImageLoader, a MIDlet that retrieves an image from the Internet and displays it on the screen.

Listing 8-1. This MIDlet retrieves an image from the Internet.

```
import java.io.*;

import javax.microedition.io.*;
import javax.microedition.lcdui.*;
import javax.microedition.midlet.*;

public class ImageLoader
    extends MIDlet {
  private Item mItem;

  public void startApp() {
    final Display display = Display.getDisplay(this);

    if (mItem == null) {
      // Put up loading progress screen.
      Form progressForm = new Form("Loading");
      display.setCurrent(progressForm);

      // Create the Form that will show the Image.
      final Form imageForm = new Form("Image");
      imageForm.addCommand(new Command("Exit", Command.EXIT, 0));
      imageForm.setCommandListener(new CommandListener() {
        public void commandAction(Command c, Displayable s) {
          notifyDestroyed();
```

```
        }
      });

      // Do network loading in a separate thread.
      Thread t = new Thread() {
        public void run() {
          try {
            String url = getAppProperty("Image-URL");
            Image image = loadImage(url);
            mItem = new ImageItem(null, image, 0, null);
          }
          catch (IOException ioe) {
            mItem = new StringItem(null, ioe.toString());
          }
          imageForm.append(mItem);
          display.setCurrent(imageForm);
        }
      };
      t.start();
    }

  }

  public Image loadImage(String url) throws IOException {
    HttpConnection hc = (HttpConnection)Connector.open(url);

    try {
      int length = (int)hc.getLength();
      byte[] data = new byte[length];
      DataInputStream in = new DataInputStream(hc.openInputStream());
      in.readFully(data);
      return Image.createImage(data, 0, data.length);
    }
    finally {
      hc.close();
    }
  }

  public void pauseApp() {}

  public void destroyApp(boolean unconditional) {}
}
```

The loadImage() method contains all of the networking code. It's fairly simple; we pass the URL of an image (retrieved as an application property) to

Connector's open() method and cast the result to HttpConnection. Then we retrieve the length of the image file, using the getLength() method. Given the length, we create a byte array and read data into it. Finally, having read the entire image file into a byte array, we can create an Image from the raw data.

You'll need to specify the MIDlet property "Image-URL" in order for this example to work correctly. Note that you need to specify the URL of a PNG image, not of a JPEG or GIF. The URL http://home.sprynet.com/~jknudsen/java2d_sm_ad.png produces the results shown in Figure 8-3.

Figure 8-3. The ImageLoader *example*

Note that this only works if the server sends back the content length, which we retrieve by calling the getLength() method of ContentConnection. The server is not required to send the content length; a more robust program would load the image file a different way if the content length were not supplied.

Posting a Form with HTTP POST

Posting a form is a little more complicated on the MIDlet side. In particular, there are request headers that need to be set in HttpConnection before the server is contacted.

You've already seen how to do a POST in Chapter 2, in the Jargoneer example. The process works like this:

1. Obtain an HttpConnection from Connector's open() method.

2. Modify the header fields of the request. In particular, you need to change the request method by calling setRequestMethod(), and you should set the "Content-Length" header by calling setRequestProperty(). This is the length of the parameters you will be sending.

3. Obtain the output stream for the HttpConnection by calling openOutputStream(). This sends the request headers to the server.

4. Send the request parameters on the output stream returned from the HttpConnection.

5. Read the response from the server from the input stream retrieved from HttpConnection's openInputStream() method.

Here it is in code, excerpted from Jargoneer.java.

```
// Obtain an HttpConnection.
HttpConnection c = null;
c = (HttpConnection)Connector.open(kURL);

// Set up the request headers.
c.setRequestMethod(HttpConnection.POST);
c.setRequestProperty("User-Agent",
    "Profile/MIDP-1.0 Configuration/CLDC-1.0");
c.setRequestProperty("Content-Language", "en-US");
c.setRequestProperty("Content-Type",
    "application/x-www-form-urlencoded");
c.setRequestProperty("Content-Length",
    String.valueOf(mPostString.length()));

// Write out the POST parameters.
out = c.openOutputStream();
out.write(mPostString.getBytes());
out.flush();

// Now read the response.
in = c.openInputStream();
```

Using Cookies for Session Tracking

HTTP is a stateless protocol, which means that each request and response pair is a separate conversation. Sometimes, though, you want the server to remember who you are. This can be done with a *session*. On the server side, a session is just a collection of information. When the client sends an HTTP request to the server, it includes a session ID as part of the request. The server can then look up the corresponding session and have some idea of the identity (or at least the state) of the client.

The most common way to store a session ID on the client side is using HTTP *cookies*. A cookie is just a little piece of data that is passed from the server to the client in an HTTP response. Most Web browsers automatically store cookies and will send them back to the appropriate server when a new request is made.

In the MIDP world, of course, there's no Web browser taking care of cookies for you. You have to do it yourself. Fortunately, it's not very complicated.

Network code that maintains a server session ID needs to do two things:

1.   When receiving a response from a server, check for a cookie. If there is a cookie present, save it away for later (perhaps in a member variable). A cookie is just another HTTP response header line. You can check for a cookie by calling getHeaderField() on an HttpConnection object after the request has been sent.

2.   When sending a request to the server, send the session ID cookie if it has been previously received. Again, sending a cookie to the server is just a matter of putting it in the request headers, using HttpConnection's setRequestProperty() method.

Each time you send a request to the server, you will be sending a session ID as a request header. The server uses this session ID to look up a session object that can be used, server side, to do useful stuff like retrieve preferences or maintain a shopping cart.

It's not hard to implement this behavior in a MIDlet. If you have a session ID cookie handy, you should send it when you open up an HTTP connection to the same server, like this:

```
HttpConnection hc = (HttpConnection)Connector.open(url);
if (mSession != null)
    hc.setRequestProperty("cookie", mSession);
```

This code assumes you have a session ID cookie saved away in the mSession member variable. The first time you contact the server, of course, you won't have a session ID cookie.

Later, when you receive a response from an HTTP request, look for a cookie. If you find one, parse out the session ID and save it away, like this:

```
InputStream in = hc.openInputStream();

String cookie = hc.getHeaderField("Set-cookie");
if (cookie != null) {
  int semicolon = cookie.indexOf(';');
  mSession = cookie.substring(0, semicolon);
}
```

The cookie string needs to be parsed because it comes in two pieces. The first piece is a path that can be used to determine when the cookie should be sent back to the server. The second part contains the session ID—that's the part we parse out and save.

Listing 8-2 shows a class, CookieMIDlet, that uses this technique to maintain a session with a server. It has a very bland user interface—just an empty Form with two commands. If you invoke the **Send** command, the MIDlet sends an HTTP request and receives a response using the cookie handling described above.

Listing 8-2. CookieMIDlet saves a server session ID cookie.

```java
import java.io.*;

import javax.microedition.io.*;
import javax.microedition.midlet.*;
import javax.microedition.lcdui.*;

public class CookieMIDlet extends MIDlet {
  private Display mDisplay;
  private Form mForm;

  private String mSession;

  public void startApp() {
    mDisplay = Display.getDisplay(this);

    if (mForm == null) {
      mForm = new Form("CookieMIDlet");

      mForm.addCommand(new Command("Exit", Command.EXIT, 0));
      mForm.addCommand(new Command("Send", Command.SCREEN, 0));
      mForm.setCommandListener(new CommandListener() {
        public void commandAction(Command c, Displayable s) {
          if (c.getCommandType() == Command.EXIT) notifyDestroyed();
          else send();
        }
      });
    }

    mDisplay.setCurrent(mForm);
  }

  private void send() {
    // Create the GET URL. Our user name and the encrypted, hex
    //   encoded message are included as parameters. The user name
    //   and base URL are retrieved as application properties.
    String url = "http://hotnoodles/midp/cookie";
```

```
  try {
    // Query the server and retrieve the response.
    HttpConnection hc = (HttpConnection)Connector.open(url);
    if (mSession != null)
      hc.setRequestProperty("cookie", mSession);
    InputStream in = hc.openInputStream();

    String cookie = hc.getHeaderField("Set-cookie");
    if (cookie != null) {
      int semicolon = cookie.indexOf(';');
      mSession = cookie.substring(0, semicolon);
    }

    int length = (int)hc.getLength();
    byte[] raw = new byte[length];
    in.read(raw);

    String s = new String(raw);
    Alert a = new Alert("Response", s, null, null);
    a.setTimeout(Alert.FOREVER);
    mDisplay.setCurrent(a, mForm);

    in.close();
    hc.close();
  }
  catch (IOException ioe) {
    Alert a = new Alert("Exception", ioe.toString(), null, null);
    a.setTimeout(Alert.FOREVER);
    mDisplay.setCurrent(a, mForm);
  }
}

public void pauseApp() {}

public void destroyApp(boolean unconditional) {}
}
```

On the server side, things are much simpler. If you're writing with servlets, you don't even have to worry about cookies. Instead, you just deal with an HttpSession object. The code that follows shows a servlet that interacts with CookieMIDlet. It's been tested on Tomcat 4.0 but should work fine on other servers. Note that you will have to map the URL used by the MIDlet to this servlet class; for details, see an introductory book on servlets or your server's documentation.

```
import javax.servlet.http.*;
import javax.servlet.*;
import java.io.*;

public class CookieServlet extends HttpServlet {
  public void doGet(HttpServletRequest request,
      HttpServletResponse response)
      throws ServletException, IOException {
    HttpSession session = request.getSession();

    String message = session.getId();

    System.out.println(message);

    response.setContentType("text/plain");
    response.setContentLength(message.length());
    PrintWriter out = response.getWriter();
    out.println(message);
  }
}
```

The servlet retrieves the HttpSession object. Then it pulls out the session ID and sends it as the response back to the MIDlet. It also prints the session ID out to the console, so you can see that the session ID on the client and is the same.

Design Tips

This section contains some suggestions about creating networked MIDlets.

- Use GET rather than POST. It's simpler, and you won't have to worry about fiddling around with the request headers.

- Don't hard-code URLs. Put them in a MIDlet property in the application descriptor. This will make it possible to change the URL without recompiling your code.

- Put network access in a separate thread. Network access always takes time; it shouldn't hold up the user interface. Furthermore, you must let your users know what's going on. Put up a "loading progress" type of message or some kind of indication that your application is trying to access a network resource.

- Make sure you handle exceptions gracefully. Network connections on wireless devices are not tremendously reliable, so you should make sure you're prepared for the worst. Catch all your exceptions and do something reasonable.

- Clean up after yourself. On a small device, resources are scarce, so be sure to close connections when you are done with them. try – finally blocks are especially useful for ensuring that unused streams and connections are closed.[1] The code in Jargoneer demonstrates this technique.

Using Datagram Connections

In this section, I'll briefly describe datagram connections. Although support for datagrams is not mandated by the MIDP specification, certain device implementations may choose to support datagram connections. Unlike stream-oriented connections, datagram connections are *connectionless*. This means that you can fire packets of data around the network, but you have no guarantee that they will reach their destination in the right order, or that they will even arrive at all.

Datagram communications is based on two interfaces in the javax.microedition.io package, DatagramConnection and Datagram. Figure 8-4 shows the methods in DatagramConnection.

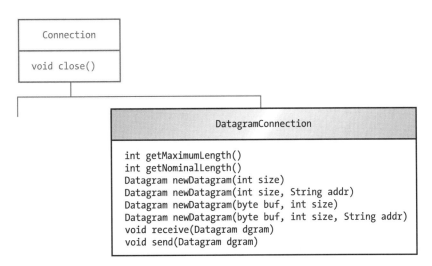

Figure 8-4. The DatagramConnection *interface*

---

1. You are probably familiar with the try – catch blocks that are used in Java for exception handling. The finally clause is not as well known, but it is very useful. Code in the finally block will be executed regardless of how control leaves the try block.

The first step is to use the generic connection framework to obtain a DatagramConnection—something like this:

```
String url = "datagram://jonathanknudsen.com:7999";
DatagramConnection dc = (DatagramConnection)Connector.open(url);
```

The URL string passed to Connector's open() method contains both the host name and port of the opposite end of the datagram connection. If datagram connections are not supported by a MIDP implementation, an exception will be thrown from the open() method.

All data is exchanged using Datagrams. To send a datagram, first ask the DatagramConnection to create one for you using one of the newDatagram() methods. Then write some data into it and pass it into the send() method of DatagramConnection. Receiving a datagram is almost as easy. You just call receive(), which blocks until a datagram is received.

In essence, Datagram is a wrapper for an array of bytes that are the payload of the datagram. You can retrieve a reference to this byte array by calling getData(). Keep in mind, however, that the data for the Datagram may be only a subset of the data in the array. You can find the array offset and length of the actual data by calling getOffset() and getLength().

Interestingly, Datagram is an extension of both the DataInput and DataOutput interfaces, so it's possible to read and write data in a Datagram as though it were a stream.

Summary

Networking on the MIDP platform is based on a generalized connection framework. The only protocol mandated by the MIDP specification is HTTP. You can perform GET, HEAD, or POST requests with just a few lines of code. HTTP session handling is also feasible. If the implementation supports it, you can also make datagram connections.

CHAPTER 9

Programming a Game Interface

Chapters 5 and 6 were devoted to MIDP's generalized user-interface APIs. Clever as these APIs are, they are unsuitable for game development and other specialized user interfaces. Games are programmed "closer to the metal" than other applications. MIDP offers a class, `javax.microedition.lcdui.Canvas`, which provides low-level access to a device's screen and input facilities. You can find out exactly which keys a user is pressing and draw whatever you want on the screen.

The Canvas Class

Canvas is the heart of MIDP's game programming API. To use it, you must create a subclass of Canvas. This differs from the Screen subclasses, which are ready to use "out of the box."

Aside from that, however, Canvas fits in very nicely with the other subclasses of Displayable. A MIDlet can mix and match regular screens and Canvases. In a game, for instance, a high score screen might be a Form, while the game itself would be played on a Canvas.

Canvas contains event-handling methods that are invoked by the MIDP implementation whenever something important happens. When the user presses a key, or when the screen needs to be painted, one of Canvas's methods will be called. Most of these methods have empty implementations in Canvas. To respond to an event, you need to override the appropriate method and provide an implementation.

The one exception to this rule is the paint() method, which is declared abstract and thus must be defined in subclasses.

Canvas Information

If you would like to draw your own user interface, you'll need some basic information about the Canvas. You can find out the size of the Canvas by calling getWidth() and getHeight(). As we'll discuss later, you can also find out the color capabilities of the device by calling methods in Display.

Canvas also features event handler methods that will be called by the MIDP implementation as your Canvas is displayed and hidden. Each time your Canvas is shown, the showNotify() method will be called. If another Displayable is shown, or the application manager decides to run a different application, hideNotify() is called.

Painting and Repainting

The MIDP implementation calls a Canvas's paint() method when the contents of the Canvas need to be shown. This paint() method should look familiar to anyone who has ever implemented a custom Swing or AWT component.

The MIDP implementation passes a Graphics object to your paint() method. Graphics has methods for drawing shapes, text, and images on a Canvas. A typical Canvas implementation, then, looks something like this:

```
import javax.microedition.lcdui.*;

public class JonathanCanvas
    extends Canvas {
  public void paint(Graphics g) {
    // Draw stuff using g.
  }
}
```

What if you want to tell the Canvas to draw itself? You can't call paint() directly, because you don't have a suitable Graphics to pass to paint(). Instead, you need to tell the MIDP implementation that it's time to paint the Canvas. The way you do this is by calling repaint(). The first version of this method simply tells Canvas to paint everything.

```
public void repaint()
public void repaint(int x, int y, int width, int height)
```

The second version is a way of saying, "I only want you to paint this rectangular portion of the screen." If the drawing you're doing is very complicated, you can save some time by only painting the portion of the Canvas that has changed. This is implemented using a technique called clipping. A later section discusses clipping in more detail.

How exactly does `repaint()` work? When you call `repaint()`, `paint()` won't be called right away. The call to `repaint()` just signals to the MIDP implementation that you want the screen to be painted. Some time later, the implementation *services* the repaint request, which results in an actual call to the `paint()` method of the `Canvas`. The MIDP implementation may even combine several repaint requests, particularly if their repaint regions overlap.

> **TIP** `Canvas` *does not automatically clear itself when you call* `repaint()`. *If you want to change what's on the screen, rather than adding to it, you should clear the screen yourself in the* `paint()` *method. You'll see how to do this in the* `FontCanvas` *example later in this chapter.*

An application can force the implementation to service all the repaint requests by calling `serviceRepaints()` on the `Canvas` object. This method does not return until all pending repaint requests have been serviced. If you are going to call `serviceRepaints()`, you should make sure that you aren't trying to acquire object locks in the `paint()` method that won't be released until `serviceRepaints()` returns. In general, you won't need to call `serviceRepaints()`; you can usually use `Display`'s `callSerially()` method instead. (See the "Multithreading and Animation" section of this chapter for a discussion of `callSerially()`.)

Drawing Shapes, Text, and Images

The `Graphics` class contains methods for drawing shapes, text, and images on a `Canvas`. It also maintains some state, like the current pen color and line style. MIDP's `Graphics` class is similar to the `Graphics` and `Graphics2D` classes in J2SE but much smaller.

Coordinate Space

All drawing on a `Canvas` takes place in a coordinate space based on the pixels of the MID. By default, the origin of this coordinate space is located in the upper-left corner of the `Canvas`. X coordinates increase in the right-hand direction, while Y coordinates increase in the downward direction, as shown in Figure 9-1.

You can adjust the origin of this coordinate space by calling the `translate()` method of the `Graphics` class. This set the origin to the given coordinates in the current coordinate system. To find out the location of the translated origin relative to the default origin, call `getTranslateX()` and `getTranslateY()`.

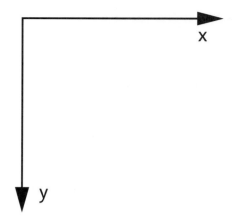

Figure 9-1. Canvas coordinate axes

Drawing and Filling Shapes

Graphics contains a collection of methods that draw and fill simple shapes. These are detailed in Table 9-1.

Table 9-1. Drawing and Filling Shapes with Graphics

SHAPE OUTLINE	FILLED SHAPE
drawLine(int x1, int y1, int x2, int y2)	-
drawRect(int x, int y, int width, int height)	fillRect(int x, int y, int width, int height)
drawRoundRect(int x, int y, int width, int height, int arcWidth, int arcHeight)	fillRoundRect(int x, int y, int width, int height, int arcWidth, int arcHeight)
drawArc(int x, int y, int width, int height, int startAngle, int arcAngle)	fillArc(int x, int y, int width, int height, int startAngle, int arcAngle)

These methods do basically what you'd expect. The following example demonstrates some simple drawing using Graphics. It consists of two pieces. First, PacerCanvas demonstrates some simple drawing and filling:

```
import javax.microedition.lcdui.*;

public class PacerCanvas
    extends Canvas {
  public void paint(Graphics g) {
    int w = getWidth();
    int h = getHeight();
```

```
    for (int x = 0; x < w; x += 10)
      g.drawLine(0, w - x, x, 0);

    int z = 30;
    g.drawRect(z, z, 20, 20);
    z += 20;
    g.fillRoundRect(z, z, 20, 20, 5, 5);
    z += 20;
    g.drawArc(z, z, 20, 20, 0, 360);
  }
}
```

The next class is Pacer, a MIDlet that uses PacerCanvas.

```
import javax.microedition.lcdui.*;
import javax.microedition.midlet.*;

public class Pacer
    extends MIDlet{
  public void startApp() {
    Displayable d = new PacerCanvas();

    d.addCommand(new Command("Exit", Command.EXIT, 0));
    d.setCommandListener(new CommandListener() {
      public void commandAction(Command c, Displayable s) {
        notifyDestroyed();
      }
    });

    Display.getDisplay(this).setCurrent(d);
  }

  public void pauseApp() {}

  public void destroyApp(boolean unconditional) {}
}
```

When you run `Pacer` in Sun's J2MEWTK emulator, it looks like Figure 9-2.

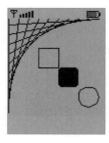

Figure 9-2. Playing around with `Graphics`

Working with Color

The `Graphics` class maintains a current drawing color that is used for drawing shape outlines, filling shapes, and drawing text. Colors are represented as combinations of red, green, and blue, with eight bits for each color component. You can set the current drawing color using the following method:

```
public void setColor(int RGB)
```

This method expects the red, green, and blue values in a packed integer, as shown in Figure 9-3.

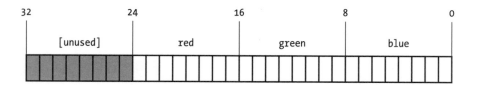

Figure 9-3. Packing a color into an integer

An alternate convenience method accepts red, green, and blue values as integers in the range from 0 to 255 inclusive:

```
public void setColor(int red, int green, int blue)
```

You can retrieve the current drawing color (as a packed integer) with `getColor()`. Alternately, you can retrieve each component separately using `getRedComponent()`, `getGreenComponent()`, and `getBlueComponent()`.

Of course, different devices will have different levels of color support, from black and white (affectionately known as "one-bit color") through full 24-bit color.

As I mentioned in Chapter 5, the isColor() and numColors() methods in Display return useful information about the capabilities of the device.

For grayscale devices, Graphics provides setGrayScale() as a convenience method. You pass it a number from 0 (black) to 255 (white). You can find out the current grayscale value by calling getGrayScale(). If the current color of this Graphics is not a grayscale color (i.e., if the red, green, and blue values of the current color are not the same), then this method returns its best guess as to the brightness of the current color.

Line Styles

Graphics also maintains a current line style, called a *stroke style*, which is used for drawing shape outlines and lines. There are two choices for line style, represented by constants in the Graphics class:

- SOLID is the default.

- DOTTED lines may also be drawn.

It's up to the implementation to decide exactly how dotted lines are implemented, so dotted lines on one device may look dashed on another. You can set or retrieve the current style using setStrokeStyle() and getStrokeStyle(). For example, the following code draws a square with a solid outline (the default) and another square with a dotted outline:

```
public void paint(Graphics g) {
  g.drawRect(20, 10, 35, 35);
  g.setStrokeStyle(Graphics.DOTTED);
  g.drawRect(20, 60, 35, 35);
}
```

Drawing Text

The Graphics class makes it easy to draw text anywhere on the screen. Text drawing is based around the idea of an anchor point. The anchor point determines exactly where the text will be drawn. Anchor points are described with a horizontal and vertical component. The Graphics class defines the horizontal and vertical anchor points as constants. Figure 9-4 illustrates the various anchor points for a string of text. Each anchor point is described as a combination of a horizontal and vertical anchor point.

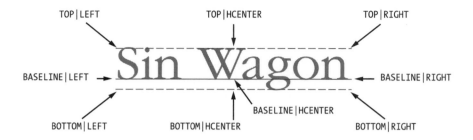

Figure 9-4. Text anchor points

To draw text, you just need to specify the text itself and the location and type of anchor point. You could, for example, place some text in the upper left corner of the screen by using a TOP | LEFT anchor point located at 0, 0.

Graphics provides four different methods for drawing text. You can draw characters or Strings, depending on what you have available:

```
public void drawChar(char character, int x, int y, int anchor)
public void drawChars(char[] data, int offset, int length,
    int x, int y, int anchor)
public void drawString(String str, int x, int y, int anchor)
public void drawSubstring(String str, int offset, int len,
    int x, int y, int anchor)
```

The following example shows how to place text at various places on a Canvas:

```
import javax.microedition.lcdui.*;

public class TextCanvas
    extends Canvas {
  public void paint(Graphics g) {
    int w = getWidth();
    int h = getHeight();

    // First label the four corners.
    g.drawString("corner", 0, 0,
        Graphics.TOP | Graphics.LEFT);
    g.drawString("corner", w, 0,
        Graphics.TOP | Graphics.RIGHT);
    g.drawString("corner", 0, h,
        Graphics.BOTTOM | Graphics.LEFT);
    g.drawString("corner", w, h,
        Graphics.BOTTOM | Graphics.RIGHT);
```

```
// Now put something in the middle (more or less).
   g.drawString("Sin Wagon", w / 2, h / 2,
       Graphics.BASELINE | Graphics.HCENTER);
  }
}
```

To see this Canvas, you'll have to create a MIDlet that displays it. I suggest using Pacer; just edit the source file so it instantiates a TextCanvas instead of a PacerCanvas. The finished product is shown in Figure 9-5.

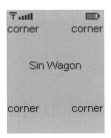

Figure 9-5. TextCanvas *in the flesh*

Note that Canvas denies us some real estate at the bottom of the screen. This is to allow space for Commands. Canvas, like any other Displayable, can display commands and have a command listener.

Selecting a Font

MIDP fonts are represented by a *font face*, *style*, and *size*. You won't find a big selection of fonts, but there are a few choices. Three faces are available, as shown in Figure 9-6. These are represented by constants in the Font class: FACE_SYSTEM, FACE_MONOSPACE, and FACE_PROPORTIONAL.

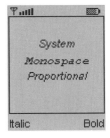

Figure 9-6. The three font faces in italics

Once you've chosen a font face, you can also specify a style and a size. The styles are what you'd expect, and they are represented by constants in the Font class: STYLE_PLAIN, STYLE_BOLD, STYLE_ITALIC, and STYLE_UNDERLINE. You can combine styles, like bold and italic, by ORing the constants together. The size is simply SIZE_SMALL, SIZE_MEDIUM, or SIZE_LARGE.

You could create a small, italic, proportional font with the following call:

```
Font f = Font.getFont(
    Font.FACE_PROPORTIONAL,
    Font.STYLE_ITALIC,
    Font.SIZE_SMALL);
```

To tell Graphics to use a new font for subsequent text, call setFont(). You can get a reference to the current font by calling getFont(). You can also find out information about a Font with the getFace(), getStyle(), and getSize() methods. For convenience, Font also includes isPlain(), isBold(), isItalic(), and isUnderlined() methods.

The MIDP implementation has a default font that you can retrieve from Font's static method getDefaultFont().

The Canvas in Listing 9-1 demonstrates the creation and use of fonts. If you'd like to play around with underlining, as well, uncomment the line in the constructor where the underlining command is added to the Canvas. If you do, you'll have more commands than will fit on the screen, so two of them will wind up in an offscreen menu.

Listing 9-1. Having fun with fonts.

```
import javax.microedition.lcdui.*;

public class FontCanvas
    extends Canvas
    implements CommandListener {
  private Font mSystemFont, mMonospaceFont, mProportionalFont;
  private Command mBoldCommand, mItalicCommand, mUnderlineCommand;

  public FontCanvas() {
    this(Font.STYLE_PLAIN);
  }

  public FontCanvas(int style) {
    setStyle(style);
    mBoldCommand = new Command("Bold", Command.SCREEN, 0);
    mItalicCommand = new Command("Italic", Command.SCREEN, 0);
    mUnderlineCommand = new Command("Underline", Command.SCREEN, 0);
    addCommand(mBoldCommand);
    addCommand(mItalicCommand);
    //addCommand(mUnderlineCommand);
    setCommandListener(this);
  }
```

```
public void setStyle(int style) {
  mSystemFont = Font.getFont(Font.FACE_SYSTEM,
      style, Font.SIZE_MEDIUM);
  mMonospaceFont = Font.getFont(Font.FACE_MONOSPACE,
      style, Font.SIZE_MEDIUM);
  mProportionalFont = Font.getFont(Font.FACE_PROPORTIONAL,
      style, Font.SIZE_MEDIUM);
}

public void paint(Graphics g) {
  int w = getWidth();
  int h = getHeight();

  // Clear the Canvas.
  g.setGrayScale(255);
  g.fillRect(0, 0, w - 1, h - 1);
  g.setGrayScale(0);
  g.drawRect(0, 0, w - 1, h - 1);

  int x = w / 2;
  int y = 20;

  y += showFont(g, "System", x, y, mSystemFont);
  y += showFont(g, "Monospace", x, y, mMonospaceFont);
  y += showFont(g, "Proportional", x, y, mProportionalFont);
}

private int showFont(Graphics g, String s, int x, int y, Font f) {
  g.setFont(f);
  g.drawString(s, x, y, Graphics.TOP | Graphics.HCENTER);
  return f.getHeight();
}

public void commandAction(Command c, Displayable s) {
  boolean isBold = mSystemFont.isBold() ^ (c == mBoldCommand);
  boolean isItalic = mSystemFont.isItalic() ^ (c == mItalicCommand);
  boolean isUnderline = mSystemFont.isUnderlined() ^
      (c == mUnderlineCommand);

  int style =
      (isBold ? Font.STYLE_BOLD : 0) |
      (isItalic ? Font.STYLE_ITALIC : 0) |
      (isUnderline ? Font.STYLE_UNDERLINED : 0);
```

115

```
        setStyle(style);
        repaint();
    }
}
```

To see this Canvas in action, you'll need a MIDlet that shows it. You could modify Pacer again, if you wish, or use the following code:

```
import javax.microedition.lcdui.*;
import javax.microedition.midlet.*;

public class FontMIDlet
    extends MIDlet
    {
  public void startApp() {
    Displayable d = new FontCanvas();

    d.addCommand(new Command("Exit", Command.EXIT, 0));
    d.setCommandListener(new CommandListener() {
      public void commandAction(Command c, Displayable s) {
        notifyDestroyed();
      }
    });

    Display.getDisplay(this).setCurrent(d);
  }

public void pauseApp() {}

  public void destroyApp(boolean unconditional) {}
}
```

Measuring Text

The Font class can tell you useful information about the dimensions of text. If you read the previous example carefully, you'll notice we already used one of these methods, getHeight(). This method returns the height of an entire line of text and can be used to position multiple lines of text.

If you really need to know the location of the baseline, call
getBaselinePosition(). This returns the distance from the top of a line
of text to the baseline. However, given the flexibility offered by the anchor
points in Graphics, you probably won't ever need to find the baseline yourself.

The rest of the methods in Font for measuring text measure the width of
various pieces of text. The names and parameters of these methods are the same
as text drawing methods in Graphics:

```
public int charWidth(char ch)
public int charsWidth(char ch, int offset, int length)
public int stringWidth(String str)
public int substringWidth(String str, int offset, int len)
```

You could draw a box around a string, for example:

```
import javax.microedition.lcdui.*;

public class BoxTextCanvas
    extends Canvas {
  private Font mFont;

  public BoxTextCanvas() {
    mFont = Font.getFont(Font.FACE_PROPORTIONAL,
        Font.STYLE_PLAIN, Font.SIZE_LARGE);
  }

  public void paint(Graphics g) {
    int w = getWidth();
    int h = getHeight();

    String s = "dolce";
    int stringWidth = mFont.stringWidth(s);
    int stringHeight = mFont.getHeight();
    int x = (w - stringWidth) / 2;
    int y = h / 2;

    g.setFont(mFont);
    g.drawString(s, x, y, Graphics.TOP | Graphics.LEFT);
    g.drawRect(x, y, stringWidth, stringHeight);
  }
}
```

Drawing Images

The Graphics class contains a single method for drawing an image:

```
public void drawImage(Image img, int x, int y, int anchor)
```

The drawImage() method uses an anchor point, just like the anchor point in the text drawing methods. The available anchor points are slightly different. BASELINE is no longer an option for the vertical anchor point of an image, as the concept of baseline is specific to text. Instead, VCENTER is an additional option for the vertical anchor point. Figure 9-7 shows the available combinations of anchor points.

Figure 9-7. Image anchor points

Clipping

Graphics maintains a rectangular *clipping shape*. The clipping shape limits drawing, such that any drawing that takes place outside of the clipping shape will not be displayed. It's kind of like painting through a stencil, except you can only use a rectangular stencil. If you were writing a game that had some kind of border on the game board, you might set the clipping rectangle to be the inside of the game board, so that no drawing could overwrite the border.

You can find out the current clipping rectangle by calling getClipX(), getClipY(), getClipWidth(), and getClipHeight().

If you would like to modify the clipping rectangle, there are two methods that you can use. First, you can set the clipping rectangle directly by calling the following method:

```
public void setClip(int x, int y, int width, int height);
```

The other possibility is to augment the current clipping rectangle with another rectangle. The following method takes the intersection of the current clipping rectangle and the supplied rectangle and uses it to set the new clipping rectangle:

```
public void clipRect(int x, int y, int width, int height);
```

Key Events

Canvas handles events at a lower level than the other Displayable subclasses. Although you can add Commands and respond to them, Canvas also includes a set of methods that handle interaction with the individual keys of a device.

The following methods are called whenever the user presses and releases a key.

```
protected void keyPressed(int keyCode)
protected void keyReleased(int keyCode)
```

The key code that is passed to these methods will most likely be one of the constants defined in Graphics, from KEY_NUM0 through KEY_NUM9 and including KEY_STAR and KEY_POUND. Devices may have more keys than this, which will be returned as device-specific key codes. Assuming there's an obvious mapping between the key and some Unicode character, the rule of thumb is that a key should have a code equal to its Unicode character value. Keys that don't have a Unicode mapping should use negative values. This means that, given a positive key code, you can find out the corresponding Unicode character by casting the int key code to char.

Note that key presses and key releases are separate events, which allows you considerable flexibility in how you design your user interface. The time between the press and the release could determine how high a game character jumps or how powerful a laser blast will be.

Depending on the device and the MIDP implementation, a key that is held down may spit out repeated key events. You can find out if repeated keys are supported by calling hasRepeatEvents(). If repeated key events are supported, the keyRepeated() method will be called with these events.

Finally, you can find a text description of a given key code by calling getKeyName().

Game Actions

Key codes may be useful in certain situations, but they're fairly specific to a device. MIDP offers a simple abstraction called a *game action* that makes it easier to map user key events to events that will be useful for games and other applications with specialized user interfaces.

The concept is simple: Supply a key code to getGameAction(), and you'll receive a game action—one of the following values: UP, DOWN, LEFT, RIGHT, FIRE, GAME_A, GAME_B, GAME_C, GAME_D. Basically game actions are a way to map the physical keys on a device to a set of video game buttons such as you might find on game platforms like Sega Genesis or Nintendo Game Boy.

To understand how this maps to a physical device, think about how you might map the UP, DOWN, LEFT, and RIGHT game actions to keys. On Sun's MIDP emulator, there are navigation keys that could easily be used for these game actions. Think about a simpler phone, however, one that has only a numeric keypad. In this case, you might want to map UP to the 2 key, DOWN to the 8 key, LEFT to the 4 key, and RIGHT to the 6 key.

Using game actions saves you from having to make these decisions yourself; the MIDP implementation simply provides a reasonable mapping for the device. To find the game action for a key code, pass the key code to getGameAction(). You can also find the key code for a game action by calling getKeyCode().

The following example listens for key presses in the keyPressed() method. It converts the key code to a game action and displays the game action on the screen.

```
import javax.microedition.lcdui.*;

public class KeyCanvas
    extends Canvas {
  private Font mFont;
  private String mMessage = "[Press keys]";
```

```
public KeyCanvas() {
  mFont = Font.getFont(Font.FACE_PROPORTIONAL,
      Font.STYLE_PLAIN, Font.SIZE_MEDIUM);
}

public void paint(Graphics g) {
  int w = getWidth();
  int h = getHeight();

  // Clear the Canvas.
  g.setGrayScale(255);
  g.fillRect(0, 0, w - 1, h - 1);
  g.setGrayScale(0);
  g.drawRect(0, 0, w - 1, h - 1);

  g.setFont(mFont);

  int x = w / 2;
  int y = h / 2;

  g.drawString(mMessage, x, y, Graphics.BASELINE | Graphics.HCENTER);
}

protected void keyPressed(int keyCode) {
  int gameAction = getGameAction(keyCode);
  switch(gameAction) {
    case UP:     mMessage = "UP";         break;
    case DOWN:   mMessage = "DOWN";       break;
    case LEFT:   mMessage = "LEFT";       break;
    case RIGHT:  mMessage = "RIGHT";      break;
    case FIRE:   mMessage = "FIRE";       break;
    case GAME_A: mMessage = "GAME_A";     break;
    case GAME_B: mMessage = "GAME_B";     break;
    case GAME_C: mMessage = "GAME_C";     break;
    case GAME_D: mMessage = "GAME_D";     break;
    default:     mMessage = ""; break;
  }
  repaint();
}
}
```

To run this example, you'll need a corresponding MIDlet to display KeyCanvas. At this point, I think you can do this by yourself.

Pointer Events

Some devices, particularly PDAs, may support a pointer. The popular Palm platform, for example, is based around the use of a stylus and touch-sensitive screen. You can find out at runtime if your device supports pointer events by calling `hasPointerEvents()` and `hasPointerMotionEvents()`. If the device supports pointer events, the following methods get called when the pointer is pressed and released:

```
protected void pointerPressed(int x, int y)
protected void pointerReleased(int x, int y)
```

If the device supports pointer motion events, the following method will be called as the user drags the stylus around the screen.

```
protected void pointerDragged(int x, int y)
```

Double Buffering

Double buffering is a well-known technique for reducing flicker in drawing and animations. Imagine you are implementing an animation that clears and redraws the entire screen for each frame of the animation. Without double buffering, the animation will flicker badly as the screen is cleared and redrawn. With double buffering, the new frame is drawn into an off-screen image (the buffer). When the off-screen drawing is complete, the image is drawn on the screen in one smooth, quick move. You pay a price in the memory that's needed for the off-screen image, but the improvement in the quality of the animation is dramatic.

The MIDP implementation may provide double buffering by default. You can find out whether a `Canvas` is double buffered by calling the `isDoubleBuffered()` method.

If the implementation does not give you double buffering, you'll have to do it yourself. Fortunately, it's not terribly difficult. The process looks like this:

1. Create an offscreen image by calling the static `Image.createImage(int width, int height)` method.

2. Obtain a `Graphics` that draws *into the image* by calling `getGraphics()` on the `Image`.

3. Draw stuff into the off-screen image using the `Graphics` object.

4. In the `paint()` method of the `Canvas`, use `drawImage()` to put the off-screen image on the `Canvas`.

Here's a Canvas subclass that creates a simple off-screen image and displays it:

```
import javax.microedition.lcdui.*;

public class OffscreenCanvas
    extends Canvas {
  private Image mImage;

  public void paint(Graphics g) {
    if (mImage == null)
      initialize();
    g.drawImage(mImage, 0, 0, Graphics.TOP | Graphics.LEFT);
  }

  private void initialize() {
    int w = getWidth();
    int h = getHeight();

    mImage = Image.createImage(w, h);

    Graphics g = mImage.getGraphics();

    g.drawRect(0, 0, w - 1, h - 1);
    g.drawLine(0, 0, w - 1, h - 1);
    g.drawLine(w - 1, 0, 0, h - 1);
  }
}
```

Multithreading and Animation

As with any graphic-interface toolkit, threading with the MIDP user-interface classes is a little tricky. The user-interface implementation has its own thread that handles both user interface methods and screen painting. For example, when the user presses a key on their device, the implementation calls keyPressed() in your Canvas subclass. The thread that calls this method belongs to the MIDP implementation. As such, it should be handled with some care. In MIDP implementations, the same thread that calls event methods also calls paint().

> **NOTE** *All event-driven user-interface toolkits have this idea of a system-owned user-interface thread. In AWT and Swing, it's called the* event dispatch thread. *The same rule applies: If you're running inside a thread that doesn't belong to you, don't take all day about it.*

Methods that are called by a thread that doesn't belong to you are *callbacks.* The rule of thumb for callbacks is that you shouldn't do anything that takes a long time. Since the thread doesn't belong to you, you shouldn't hold it up a long time performing your work. Because this thread is responsible for operating the user interface, holding it up with lengthy computations will make your application look lobotomized. Suppose, for example, that you had to retrieve some data from the network. In response to a Command, you might do something like this:

```
public void commandAction(Command c, Displayable s) {
  if (c == mNetworkCommand) {
    // Create a progress screen, progressScreen.
    mDisplay.setCurrent(progressForm);
    // Now do the network stuff.
    // Oops! Users never see progressScreen.
  }
  // ...
}
```

The problem is that the progress screen won't be shown. The commandAction() method is called from the user-interface thread, the same thread that's responsible for painting the screen. If you tie up this thread with some lengthy processing of your own, the user-interface thread never has a chance to update the screen. If you need to do something that takes a long time, create a separate thread for it. In the Jargoneer example in Chapter 2, for example, network access was performed in a separate thread.

In certain situations, you will need to ask the user-interface thread to execute code on your behalf. If you are showing an animation, for example, you'll want to make sure that the frames of the animation are properly synchronized with the repainting cycle. Otherwise, you're likely to end up showing frames that are partially drawn.

Display has a mechanism for executing your code in the user-interface thread. It has a method, callSerially(), that accepts a Runnable. When the user-interface thread is ready, meaning when it has finished servicing all repaint requests, it will execute the run() method of the Runnable from the user-interface thread. A typical animation, then, looks like this:

```
public class AnimationCanvas
    extends Canvas
    implements Runnable {
  public start() {
    run();
  }
```

```
public void paint(Graphics g) {
  // Paint a frame of the animation.
}

public void run() {
  // Update our state.
  // Now request a paint of the new frame.
  repaint();
  Display.callSerially(this);
  }
}
```

You'd kick off the animation by calling start(), which in turn would simply call run(). Inside run(), we update our state, call repaint() to request the painting of a new frame. Then we use callSerially() to request that we get called again when the painting is done.

The following example demonstrates this technique. It consists of two classes, Sweep and SweepCanvas. Sweep is a MIDlet that displays the class that actually implements the animation, SweepCanvas. The running SweepCanvas is shown in Figure 9-8.

Figure 9-8. SweepCanvas *animation running on a grayscale emulator*

This example breaks tradition from the other Canvas examples in this chapter in two regards. First, notice that the animation must be explicitly started. Sweep accomplishes this by calling SweepCanvas's start() method. Furthermore, we need to pass a reference to the MIDlet's Display to SweepCanvas. SweepCanvas uses this reference to make the connection to callSerially() to drive the animation along.

First, here's the source code for Sweep:

```java
import javax.microedition.lcdui.*;
import javax.microedition.midlet.*;

public class Sweep
    extends MIDlet
    {
  public void startApp() {
    Display display = Display.getDisplay(this);

    SweepCanvas sweeper = new SweepCanvas(display);
    sweeper.start();

    sweeper.addCommand(new Command("Exit", Command.EXIT, 0));
    sweeper.setCommandListener(new CommandListener() {
      public void commandAction(Command c, Displayable s) {
        notifyDestroyed();
      }
    });

    display.setCurrent(sweeper);
  }

  public void pauseApp() {}

  public void destroyApp(boolean unconditional) {}
}
```

And here's the code for SweepCanvas:

```java
import javax.microedition.lcdui.*;

public class SweepCanvas
    extends Canvas
    implements Runnable {
  private boolean mTrucking;
  private int mTheta;
  private int mBorder;
  Display mDisplay;
```

```
public SweepCanvas(Display display) {
  mTrucking = true;
  mTheta = 0;
  mBorder = 10;
  mDisplay = display;
}

public void start() {
  run();
}

public void stop() {
  mTrucking = false;
}

public void paint(Graphics g) {
  int width = getWidth();
  int height = getHeight();

  // Clear the Canvas.
  g.setGrayScale(255);
  g.fillRect(0, 0, width - 1, height - 1);
  g.setGrayScale(0);

  int x = mBorder;
  int y = mBorder;
  int w = width - mBorder * 2;
  int h = height - mBorder * 2;
  for (int i = 0; i < 8; i++) {
    g.setGrayScale((7 - i) * 32);
    g.fillArc(x, y, w, h, mTheta + i * 10, 10);
    g.fillArc(x, y, w, h, (mTheta + 180) % 360 + i * 10, 10);
  }
}

public void run() {
  mTheta = (mTheta + 1) % 360;
  repaint();
  if (mTrucking == true) mDisplay.callSerially(this);
}
}
```

Summary

We've covered a lot of ground in this chapter. The Canvas class provides a low-level interface for games or other demanding applications. You can draw shapes, text, and images on a Canvas using the Graphics class. Furthermore, you can receive detailed input information about which keys the user is pressing. Game actions are a simple generalized input method based on key events. Finally, you should understand the multithreading issues with repainting and event callbacks. Lengthy processing should be placed a separate thread so it doesn't bring the system-owned user-interface thread to a grinding halt. Animations can use Display's callSerially() method to synchronize with the user-interface thread.

CHAPTER 10

Performance Tuning

MIDP is a small platform. The processor on the MID will probably be much slower than a typical desktop computer processor, and the available memory will be much smaller also. Making your application run fast and lean is important. You'll need to use memory sparingly, make your application run fast enough to be easily usable, and structure it so that the code itself is as small as it can be.

This chapter describes simple methods for benchmarking your existing code. It then goes on to describe various optimizations that can make your code run faster or use less memory. Common sense will take you a long way, but this chapter is devoted to giving you the basic techniques for optimizing your application.

The important rule of thumb is this: only optimize where it's needed. Said another way: if it ain't broke, don't fix it. I suggest that your first pass at coding your application should concentrate on cleanliness and maintainability. If there are performance problems, identify them and begin optimizing. You shouldn't be optimizing code as you write it—that's just likely to result in hard-to-read, hard-to-maintain code. Write first, then test, then optimize.

Benchmarking

In the J2SE world, there are many tools for examining the performance of code, the location of bottlenecks, and memory usage. Unfortunately, none of this is available in the J2ME world (as of this writing). You'll have to perform benchmarking the old-fashioned way. For this, there are several methods in the MIDP API that will be useful. To test memory use, you can use the following methods in `java.lang.Runtime`:

```
public long freeMemory()
public long totalMemory()
```

The first method tells how much memory, in bytes, is currently available. The second method gives the total number of bytes in the current runtime environment, whether they are used for objects or not. Interestingly, this number can change, as the host environment (device operating system) can give more memory to the Java runtime environment.

To find out how much memory an object uses, you can do something like this:

```
Runtime runtime = Runtime.getRuntime();
long before, after;
System.gc();
before = runtime.freeMemory();
Object newObject = new String();
after = runtime.freeMemory();
long size = before - after;
```

Aside from examining memory usage, you may also be concerned with the speed of your application. Again, you can test this the old-fashioned way—look at the clock before you start doing something, then look at it again when you're finished. The relevant method comes from the `java.lang.System` class:

```
public static long currentTimeMillis()
```

You might calculate the execution time for a method like this:

```
long start, finish;
start = System.currentTimeMillis();
someMethod();
finish = System.currentTimeMillis();
long duration = finish - start;
```

Optimizing Memory Use

It's easy for J2SE programmers to be blasé about memory usage. After all, having a garbage collector means you don't have to worry about explicitly freeing memory—objects that are no longer in use will be magically harvested by the garbage collector, running in a low-priority thread. In the J2ME universe, however, memory is scarce and should be treated with respect. Furthermore, both the allocation of memory and the work of the garbage collector can drag down the speed of your application. In this section, we'll look at techniques for efficient object use, particularly with `Strings` and `StringBuffers`. Finally, I'll talk about gracefully handling the situation where there really isn't any memory left.

Creating and Discarding Objects

If you're creating a new object inside a loop, it should be setting off alarm bells in your head. Every time you create an object (using new), memory is allocated. Allocating memory takes time. Worse, objects created at the beginning of a loop are likely to fall out of scope by the end of the loop, which means that each iteration through the loop pushes the runtime system closer to running the garbage collector. Here's an example:

```
// Set up the inputs and results arrays.
Object[] inputs = new Object[0];
int[] results = new int[0];
// Process each input to calculate a result.
int length = inputs.length;
for (int i = 0; i < length; i++) {
  Processor p = new Processor(inputs[i]);
  results[i] = p.calculateResult();
}
```

Creating objects in a loop imposes a double penalty in terms of performance. You pay a price up front when the object is first created, then later when the object is garbage collected.

You can almost always restructure your code to avoid this problem. For example, instead of creating a new Processor for each input, you could do something like this:

```
// Set up the inputs and results arrays.
Object[] inputs = new Object[0];
int[] results = new int[0];
// Process each input to calculate a result.
int length = inputs.length;
Processor p = new Processor();
for (int i = 0; i < length; i++) {
  p.setInput(inputs[i]);
  results[i] = p.calculateResult();
}
```

Strings *and* StringBuffers

Strings have a special status in Java. They are the only objects for which the plus operator '+' is overloaded. Each time you concatenate strings using the plus operator, be wary—behind the scenes, new String and StringBuffer objects are probably being created for you.

String and StringBuffer share a curious relationship. When you can create and modify a StringBuffer, the actual work is performed on an internal character array. When you create a String from the StringBuffer, the String points to the same character array. Everything is fine so far, right? But if you further modify the StringBuffer, it cleverly creates a new character array, a copy of the old one. Thus, while StringBuffer is generally an efficient way to create Strings, it is not always obvious exactly when new objects are created.

The moral of the story is that every place you see string concatenation, there may be new objects being created. If you're assembling strings inside a loop, you should think about a different approach, possibly involving StringBuffer. Another possible optimization is to forego String and StringBuffer entirely and just use character arrays. While this may be a fast and efficient solution in your own code, keep in mind that many APIs require Strings as parameters and return Strings from methods, so you may end up doing a lot of conversion between character arrays and Strings.

Failing Gracefully

Given the paucity of memory in a typical MID, your application should be prepared for disappointment each time it asks for memory. Each time objects are created, your code should catch java.lang.OutOfMemoryError. It is far better for you to catch OutOfMemoryErrors than for your host environment to catch them. You, at least, have a chance to do something reasonable—free up some memory and try again, or fail gracefully with a politely worded message to the user. The host environment is not likely to be so kind, and user perception of your application will be much worse.

Coding for Speed

Small devices have small, relatively slow processors. Part of your task as a developer is ensuring that your application runs fast enough that users won't reject it.

Optimize Loops

One simple optimization has to do with looping. A typical loop through a Vector v might look like this:

```
for (int i = 0; i < v.size(); i++) {
  Object o = v.elementAt(i);
  // Process the Object o.
}
```

Each time through the loop, v's size() method is called. An optimized version would store the size of the vector first, like this:

```
int size = v.size();
for (int i = 0; i < size; i++) {
  Object o = v.elementAt(i);
  // Process the Object o.
}
```

This is a simple example, but it illustrates that loop conditions are one place you can look for speed optimizations.

Use Arrays Instead of Objects

Arrays are usually faster and leaner than collection classes. We touched on this theme earlier in our discussion of Strings and StringBuffers; if it's not too clumsy, using character arrays directly will probably be more efficient than dealing with String and StringBuffer objects. The same rule applies to the MIDP collection classes Vector and Hashtable. Although Vector and Hashtable are simple and convenient, they do impose some overhead that can be trimmed. Vector is basically just a wrapper for an array, so if you can work with an array directly, you'll save yourself some memory and processing time. Similarly, if you have a simple mapping of key objects to value objects, it might make sense to use object arrays instead of Hashtable.

If you do decide to use Hashtable or Vector, try to size them correctly when you create them. Both Vector and Hashtable grow larger as needed, but it is relatively expensive. Vector creates a new internal array and copies elements from the old array to the new array. Hashtable allocates new arrays and performs a computationally expensive operation called *rehashing*. Both Vector and Hashtable have constructors that allow you to specify the initial size of the collection. You should specify the initial size of these collections as accurately as possible.

If you are using the persistent storage APIs, you may be tempted to wrap stream classes around the record data. For example, you might read a record, then wrap a `ByteArrayInputStream` around the record's data, and then wrap a `DataInputStream` around the `ByteArrayInputStream` to read primitive types from the record. This is likely too heavy to be practical. If at all possible, work directly with the record's byte array.

Use Buffered I/O

Don't read bytes one at a time from a stream, and don't write them out one at a time. Although the stream classes provide methods that read and write a single byte, you should avoid them if at all possible. It will almost always be more efficient to read or write a whole array full of data.

J2SE provides `BufferedReader` and `BufferedWriter` classes that provide buffering functionality "for free." There is no such luxury in the MIDP universe, so if you want to use buffering, you'll have to do it yourself.

Be Clean

One simple piece of advice is to clean up after yourself. Releasing resources as soon as you are done with them can improve the performance of your application. If you have internal arrays or data structures, you should free them when you're not using them. One way to do this is to set your array reference to `null` so the array can be garbage collected. You could even call the garbage collector explicitly with `System.gc()` if you're anxious to release memory back to the runtime system.

Network connections should also be released as soon as you're done with them. One good way to do this is to use a `finally` clause. Consider the following code, which does not use a `finally` clause:

```
HttpConnection hc = null;
InputStream in = null;
try {
  hc = (HttpConnection)Connector.open(url);
  in = hc.openInputStream();
  // Read data from in.
  in.close();
  hc.close();
}
catch (IOException ioe) {
  // Handle the exception.
}
```

The problem occurs if an exception is thrown while you're trying to read data from the connection's input stream. In this case, execution jumps down to the exception handler, and the input stream and connection are never closed. In a J2SE environment, with memory to burn, this is probably not a big deal. But on a MID, a hanging connection could be a disaster. When you absolutely, positively want to be sure to run some code, you should put it in a finally block like this:

```
HttpConnection hc = null;
InputStream in = null;
try {
  hc = (HttpConnection)Connector.open(url);
  in = hc.openInputStream();
  // Read data from in.
}
catch (IOException ioe) {
  // Handle the exception.
}
finally {
  try {
    if (in != null) in.close();
    if (hc != null) hc.close();
  }
  catch (IOException ioe) {}
}
```

This is starting to look a little ugly, particularly the try and catch inside our finally block. A cleaner solution would be to enclose this code in a method and declare that the method throws IOException. This cleans up the code considerably:

```
private void doNetworkStuff(String url) throws IOException {
  HttpConnection hc = null;
  InputStream in = null;
  try {
    hc = (HttpConnection)Connector.open(url);
    in = hc.openInputStream();
    // Read data from in.
  }
  finally {
    if (in != null) in.close();
    if (hc != null) hc.close();
  }
}
```

The deal with `finally` is that its code gets executed no matter how control leaves the try block. If an exception is thrown, or if somebody calls `return`, or even if control leaves the `try` block normally, our `finally` block still gets executed. Note that there is still small room for trouble here: if an exception is thrown when we try to close `in`, then `hc` will never be closed. You could enclose each `close()` call in its own `try` and `catch` block to handle this problem.

Optimize the User Interface

It's important to remember that you are trying to optimize the *perceived* speed of your application, not the actual speed of the application. Users get fidgety if the application freezes up for a few seconds; adding some sort of progress indicator can go a long way toward making users happier. There's really nothing you can do to make the network run faster, but if you display a spinning clock or a moving progress bar, your application will at least look like it's still alive while it's waiting for the network.

Keep in mind that users of mobile phones and other small "consumer" devices will be much more demanding than typical desktop computer users. Through years of experience, bitter desktop computer users have fairly low expectations of their applications. They realize that most desktop applications have a learning curve and are frequently cantankerous. Consumer devices, on the other hand, are much more likely to work right the first time, requiring neither manuals nor advanced degrees to operate.

With this in mind, be sure that your MIDlet user interface is uncomplicated, fast, responsive, and informative.

Optimizing Application Deployment

One last area of optimization has to do with the actual deployment of your application. As you may remember from Chapter 3, MIDlets are packaged in MIDlet suites, which are really just fancy JAR files. One way to optimize your application is partition your classes so that only the ones you need are loaded into the runtime environment. If you are careful, you can reduce the size or your MIDlet suite JAR by eliminating classes you don't need. Finally, a code obfuscator may be used to further reduce the size or the MIDlet suite JAR.

Partition Your Application

The MIDP runtime environment loads classes as they are needed. You can use this to your advantage to optimize the runtime footprint of your application. For example, suppose you write a datebook application that has the capability to send you reminder e-mails, or *ticklers*. You would probably realize that many people will not take advantage of the tickler feature. Why should they have the tickler code taking up space in their MID if they're not using ticklers? If you partition your code correctly, all of the tickler functionality can be encapsulated in a single class. If the rest of the application never calls the tickler code, the class will not be loaded, resulting in a slimmer runtime footprint.

Only Include Classes You Need

You may be using third-party packages in your MIDlet suite, like an XML parser (see Chapter 11) or a cryptography package (see Chapter 12). For development, you might have simply dumped the whole package into your MIDlet suite. But come deployment time, you should prune out the excess packages to reduce the size or your MIDlet suite JAR. In some cases this will be fairly easy, like dumping out WAP support classes if you're simply parsing XML. Other times it will not be so obvious which classes you need and which ones you can get rid of. However, if you really want to reduce your MIDlet suite JAR size, this is a crucial step.

Use an Obfuscator

Finally, a *bytecode obfuscator* can reduce the size of your class files. A bytecode obfuscator is a tool that is supposed to make it difficult to decompile class files. Decompilation is a process by which someone can recreate the source code that was used to make a particular class file. People who are worried about competitors stealing their code use obfuscators to make decompilation more difficult. However, obfuscation has the side effect of reducing class file size, mainly because the descriptive method and variable names you created are replaced with small machine-generated names. If you're very serious about reducing the size of your MIDlet suite JAR, try obfuscating your code. I suggest running the obfuscator before preverifying the class files, but it's conceivable it would work the other way around, too. Here are two obfuscators to get you started:

```
http://www.retrologic.com/retroguard-main.html
http://www.alphaWorks.ibm.com/tech/JAX
```

Summary

MIDP applications are targeted to run on a small platform, which means that using memory and processing power efficiently is important. Creating and destroying objects is expensive, so one way to optimize your code is to reduce the number of objects you create. One common source of new objects is code that creates Strings. Consider optimizing String manipulation using StringBuffer or character arrays. Similarly, you may be able to streamline code by using object arrays in place of Vectors or Hashtables. Remember that performance is as much about perception as anything else; provide a responsive, active user interface and handle failures gracefully. You can also optimize the delivery of your application in several ways. First, partitioning the functionality of your application intelligently can reduce the runtime footprint of your application. Next, trimming out excess classes can reduce the size of your MIDlet suite JAR. Finally, a bytecode obfuscator can further reduce the size of your MIDlet suite JAR.

CHAPTER 11

Parsing XML

On the desktop and in the enterprise, Java and XML is a winning combination. In brief, Java is portable code and XML is portable data. Developing in Java gives you the ability to deploy code on many different platforms, while XML supplies a highly portable data format for exchanging data between application components and applications themselves.

XML's popularity is sure to reach into the J2ME world. This chapter describes XML parsers that are available for MIDP environments. This is fun stuff, right at the raw edge of J2ME development. MIDP is new enough that things like XML parsers haven't been fully ported to the platform, and you will probably have to mess around with the source code for these parsers to get them to run.

XML Overview

XML is the Extensible Markup Language. An XML file is some collection of data that is demarcated by tags. XML files are structured and highly portable.

Let's consider the Jargoneer application from Chapter 2 again. In that application, the MIDP device requests an HTML page from the Jargon File server, then parses the page and displays the results on the screen. As I mentioned, a cleaner architecture might be to have the MIDP device talk to an intermediate server. This server would retrieve the HTML page, perform the parsing, and send some distilled version of the data down to the MIDP device. Figure 11-1 shows this architecture.

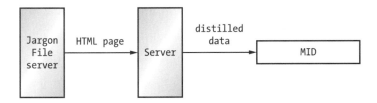

Figure 11-1. A simple architecture for Jargoneer

What, exactly, would get sent from the intermediate server to the MIDP device? The simplest technique for exchanging data between a server and a device would be to use a properties file, like this:

```
word: grok
pronunciation: /grok/
type: vt.
meaning: [from the novel "Stranger in ...
```

This works fine and is probably all you would need for simple applications. You'd have to write a class that could parse this input (MIDP doesn't include `java.util.Properties`), but that wouldn't be too bad.

However, chances are excellent that some parts of your application are already speaking XML, and it would likely simplify your life considerably if your MIDlet could parse XML instead of having its own specific data format. Furthermore, using XML validation during the development cycle may be a big help in flushing out bugs.

As an XML file, then, the same information would probably look like this:

```
<?xml version="1.0" encoding="ISO-8859-1"?>
<jargon-definition>
  <word>grok</word>
  <pronunciation>/grok/</pronunciation>
  <type>vt.</type>
  <meaning>[from the novel "Stranger in ...</meaning>
</jargon-definition>
```

This simple XML document illustrates some important points. First, tags mark off every piece of data (element) in the document. In essence, every element has a name. Matching start and end tags are used to clearly separate elements. For example, the start tag `<word>` and the end tag `</word>` surround the word itself. Also note that elements may be nested. The `jargon-definition` element is simply a collection of other elements. Any of the other elements could contain further nested elements.

Element tags may also contain attributes. An alternate way of writing the previous XML file looks like this:

```
<?xml version="1.0" encoding="ISO-8859-1"?>
<jargon-definition word="grok" pronunciation="/grok/" type="vt.">
  [from the novel "Stranger in ...
</jargon-definition>
```

It's up to you exactly how you structure your XML data. Usually it depends on the structure of your application and the systems with which you will be exchanging data.

XML and HTML

XML looks a lot like HTML, but there are some important differences. First, HTML has a fixed set of tags, like <TITLE>, <BODY>, <H1>, <P>, and so forth. In XML, you can define whatever tags you want.

HTML is also pretty lax about requiring closing tags. For example, HTML documents typically have <P> tags at the beginning of each paragraph, but it's unusual to have matching </P> close tags. As a matter of fact, the HTML world is pretty loose about document formatting in general. You can throw all sorts of strange documents at a browser and it will do its best to display them.

It is possible to write HTML such that it complies with XML; this is XHTML. For more information on XHTML, see http://www.w3.org/TR/xhtml1/.

Understanding SAX

SAX is the Simple API for XML, a standard API for Java applications that want to parse XML data. The API is documented online at http://www.megginson.com/SAX/, but SAX-compliant parsers usually include the SAX API as part of their software. The current version of SAX is 2.0, but the small parsers covered in this chapter are only at the 1.0 level if they implement SAX at all.

SAX 1.0 revolves around the org.xml.sax.Parser interface. Parser has a method, parse(), that parses through an entire XML document, spitting out events to listening objects. Typically, your application will implement a DocumentHandler that receives notification about start tags, end tags, element data, and other important events. A SAX 1.0 application looks something like this:

```
try {
  Parser p = new SAXParser(); // Create a specific parser implementation.
  // Create some DocumentHandler named handler.
  p.setDocumentHandler(handler);
  p.parse();
}
catch (Exception e) { // Handle exceptions. }
```

The call to parse() proceeds until the document has been fully parsed. During the parse, callback methods in the registered DocumentHandler are invoked. In these methods, you'll process the data from the XML document.

SAX 1.0 is not MIDP compliant straight out of the box. The Parser interface includes a setLocale() method that references the java.util.Locale class, a class that is missing in the MIDP platform. Later sections on MinML and wbxml describe how to work around this problem.

Another standard API, the Document Object Model (DOM), takes a different approach to XML parsing. With DOM, the parser creates an internal model of a document as it is parsed. After parsing is complete, an application can examine the entire document. DOM is further described here at http://www.w3.org/TR/DOM-Level-2-Core/. Although none of the parsers described in this chapter implement DOM directly, some of them do follow the DOM paradigm of creating an internal representation of a parsed document.

Validation and Development Cycle

XML documents may also make reference to a Document Type Definition (DTD) or an XML Schema; these are files that describe the contents of a particular kind of XML document. We could, for example, write a DTD that specified the contents of a jargon-definition document. This is part of the power of XML, and it's the reason XML is sometimes called *self-describing data*.

Given a document, you can determine if it conforms to its DTD, which is a great way to determine if part of your system is producing data that's unreadable by the rest of your system. In XML terms, a document that follows the rules of its DTD or schema is *valid*. In the J2SE and J2EE worlds, parsers may be validating or non-validating. The J2ME world is too small to support XML document validation, so all of the parsers we'll discuss in this chapter are non-validating.

Even though you won't be able to perform validation on a MID, you may well want to use validating parsers during your development and test cycle. For example, you might write code that emulates the MID client, having it request data from your server and validate the results. This helps flush out bugs in the server code before you make the switchover to the MID client software.

Design Tips

Common sense, as always, takes you a long way. As you contemplate the use of XML in your MIDP application, keep three things in mind:

- Keep the documents small. If you're sending some 100-KB document down to the MID and only using a few elements, it's time to rethink your server-side strategy. You can probably transform the document at the server and just send what you need to the MID. Keep in mind that network connectivity is likely to be slow, and there's not much memory on the MID.

- Don't use comments in the XML that you send to the MID, except perhaps as a debugging aid during the development cycle. Comments will only make the document longer, which implies a slower download and more memory usage on the MID.

- Choose a parser that fits your needs. Some of the parsers we'll examine build an entire model of a document in memory as the document is parsed. This is like writing a blank check to the supplier of the XML document. If the server sends you a 1-MB file, these types of parsers will attempt to read through the whole thing, right up until they run out of memory. On the other hand, if you know the size of the files you'll be parsing, and they are small enough, you might choose a model-building parser, as it is slightly easier to use than the other types of parsers.

Finally, you may be concerned about the performance of a small XML parser. This is a valid concern, especially on a small device that has a relatively slow processor. For a fascinating comparison of XML parser performance, see `http://www.extreme.indiana.edu/~aslom/exxp/`. With small documents, the small parsers can hold their own or outperform larger parsers.

MIDP XML Parser Roundup

Table 11-1 lists small XML parsers that can be used with the MIDP platform. Each parser will be explored in subsequent sections, but the table here gives you a quick way of comparing parsers. Each of these parsers is released under some type of open-source software license as listed in the License column. The Size column shows the approximate size of the compressed class files for the parser. The Type column describes the parsing paradigm using one of the following:

- "Pull" indicates that the programmer repeatedly calls a method on the parser to propel it through a document.

- "Push" means that the parser runs through the entire document by itself, invoking callback methods in your code when important events happen. SAX parsers implement the push paradigm.

- "Model" indicates that the parser builds some internal representation (in memory) of the document. After parsing is finished, your code can examine this model and pull out element data.

The MIDP column indicates whether or not the parser source code compiles without modification on the MIDP platform. Finally, the SAX column tells what version of SAX the parser supports.

Table 11-1. Small XML Parsers

NAME	URL	LICENSE	SIZE	MIDP	TYPE	SAX
kXML	http://kxml.enhydra.org/	EPL	34KB	yes	pull	no
MinML	http://www.wilson.co.uk/xml/minml.htm	BSD	13KB	no	push	1.0
NanoXML	http://nanoxml.sourceforge.net/	zlib/libpng	10KB	patch	model	1.0 optional
TinyXML	http://www.gibaradunn.srac.org/tiny/	GPL	13KB	no	model	no
wbxml	http://www.trantor.de/wbxml/	GPL	19KB	no	push	1.0

Table 11-2 provides more information about each type of license, listing both the license name and a URL that provides more information.

Table 11-2. Software Licenses

NAME	URL
EPL	http://kxml.enhydra.org/software/license/
BSD	http://www.opensource.org/licenses/bsd-license.html
zlib/libpng	http://www.opensource.org/licenses/zlib-license.html
GPL	http://www.gibaradunn.srac.org/tiny/gpl.txt

In the following sections, I'll describe each parser. I'll explain how to make the parser compile for MIDP, as well as how each parser can be used from a MIDlet.

kXML

kXML is the largest and most complete parser I'll cover. Originally developed at the Universität Dortmund in Germany, it is now part of the Enhydra Web site. It is based on Common XML (`http://simonstl.com/articles/cxmlspec.txt`), which is a set of recommendations for using XML 1.0. Common XML specifies a core set of XML functionality and is really more of a state of mind than a specification.

kXML is specifically designed for KVM environments like CLDC and MIDP. Of the five parsers covered in this chapter, kXML is the only one that compiles without modification in a MIDP environment. It is also the largest; if you're concerned about memory, you might want to consider one of the other parsers, which are considerably smaller.

kXML implements a pull-based parser that is contained in the de.kxml.parser package. *Pull-based* means that you tell the parser to parse each element. A SAX parser, by contrast, parses the whole document in one shot and just lets you know when things happen.

Most of kXML's parser functionality is defined in the abstract Parser class. In your code, you will use the concrete DefaultParser subclass. The basic idea is to instantiate a DefaultParser, passing in a java.io.Reader that represents the data to be parsed. Then call the read() method repeatedly, processing each element until the end of the document is reached. read() returns a ParseEvent, which could represent a start tag, element text, or other parser events. In MIDlet code, it looks something like this:

```
String filename = "example1.xml";
InputStream rawIn = this.getClass().getResourceAsStream(filename);
Reader in = new InputStreamReader(rawIn);
try {
  Parser p = new DefaultParser(in);
  ParseEvent pe = null;
  while ((pe = p.read()) != null) {
    ; // Process the event.
    if (pe.getType() == de.kxml.Xml.END_DOCUMENT)
      break;
  }
}
catch (IOException ioe) {
  // Handle the exception.
}
```

ParseEvent has a type property (returned by getType()) that will be one of the constants defined in the de.kxml.Xml class. ParseEvent also has various subclasses that represent some of the event types. However, downcasting will rarely be necessary as ParseEvent already contains most of the methods you need for accessing data.

In the previous sample code, we've explicitly tested for an END_DOCUMENT event type that signals that the parser is finished.

How to Build a Parser

The process for building an XML parser in MIDP is surprisingly easy. I used the Java 2, Micro Edition Wireless Toolkit (J2MEWTK) from Sun. The source code for all the parsers is readily available. All you have to do is copy the source code into one of the J2MEWTK project directories. For example, the MinML parser has two directories of source code, *org* and *uk*, containing the SAX source code and the MinML source code, respectively. Using the J2MEWTK, I created a new project called MinMLproject. J2MEWTK created a new directory, *<J2MEWTK>/apps/MinMLproject/src*. I just copied the MinML source code into this directory. Inside J2MEWTK, I pressed the Build button, which compiled all the source code.

If you make the modifications as described in this chapter, you can get MinML to compile without errors. Then just add some MIDlet code and you're ready to go. J2MEWTK will automatically package the MinML classes with your MIDlet classes to make a MIDlet suite JAR.

MinML

MinML implements the SAX 1.0 APIs, but this means that it won't build and run on MIDP without some modification. In this section, I'll describe how to get MinML to build on MIDP. Then we'll take a look at how to use MinML from a MIDlet.

One important limitation of MinML is that it does not support *mixed content*, an element that contains both character data and other elements. Without mixed content, elements contain either character data or they contain other elements. For example, the following element contains character data:

```
<text>excuse me but can I be you for a while</text>
```

By contrast, the following "text" element contains both character data and another element, "italic":

```
<text>excuse me but can I <italic>be you for a while</italic></text>
```

Our approach to making MinML build on MIDP will be to supply missing classes. MinML expects to find two classes, `java.util.Locale` and `java.net.URL`, that are not present on the MIDP platform. Rather than modifying the MinML source code (also a valid approach), we will supply dummy implementations of these two classes. First, we can supply an empty implementation for `java.util.Locale`:

```
package java.util;
public class Locale {
}
```

If you're using J2MEWTK for development, simply save this file as *Locale.java* in the *<J2MEWTK>/apps/<projectname>/src/java/util* directory. You can follow a similar process for `java.net.URL`:

```
package java.net;
import java.io.InputStream;
public class URL {
  public URL(String url) {}
  public InputStream openStream() { return null; }
}
```

Save this code in *<J2MEWTK>/apps/<projectname>/src/java/net*. Now MinML should compile without errors.

To actually use the parser, you will most likely extend `uk.co.wilson.xml.MinML`, which implements the `org.xml.sax.Parser` interface. In addition, `MinML` also implements the `DocumentHandler` interface. You might, therefore, create a `MinML` instance and override the `DocumentHandler` methods in which you are interested. The following code illustrates this technique:

```
String filename = "example1.xml";
InputStream rawIn = this.getClass().getResourceAsStream(filename);
Reader in = new InputStreamReader(rawIn);
try {
  MinML p = new MinMLSubclass();
  p.parse(in);
}
catch (Exception e) { // Handle exceptions. }
```

As the file is parsed, the `DocumentHandler` methods in your `MinMLSubclass` instance will be called. If you override `DocumentHandler` methods like `startElement()`, `characters()`, and others, you can get callbacks for the information that you need.

NanoXML

NanoXML, like MinML, does not support mixed content. Although the basic download does not compile in the MIDP environment, Eric Giguere has ported NanoXML to the CLDC. A modified source file is available from http://nanoxml.sourceforge.net/kvm.html.

Building NanoXML on MIDP is a matter of substituting Eric Giguere's *kXMLElement.java* for the *XMLElement.java* that comes with NanoXML.

NanoXML follows the DOM model, where an entire document is read into memory and can be examined later. Parsing the document is a matter of creating an instance of kXMLElement and calling one of its parse methods. There are methods for parsing Strings, character arrays, and Readers. In a MIDlet you could parse a file like this:

```
String filename = "example1.xml";
InputStream rawIn = this.getClass().getResourceAsStream(filename);
Reader in = new InputStreamReader(rawIn);
try {
  kXMLElement p = new kXMLElement();
  p.parseFromReader(in);
}
catch (Exception e) { // Handle exceptions. }
```

Once the document is fully parsed, you can examine its contents using getChildren() or enumerateChildren() methods, which return collections of nested kXMLElements.

NanoXML also offers the possibility of modifying a document and writing it back out to a stream. This is probably not very useful on a MIDP device, but it's an interesting possibility nevertheless.

TinyXML

TinyXML also follows the DOM model of parsing an entire document into some internal representation. It will not compile directly on MIDP, however, and requires some modifications to the source code itself. In the gd.xml.XMLParser source code, the following changes will result in MIDP-compliant code:

1. Create local static methods `isLetter()` and `isLetterOrDigit()` as follows:

```
private static boolean isLetter(char c) {
    return (c >= 'a' && c <= 'z') ||
        (c >= 'A' && c <= 'Z') ||
        c == ':' ||
        c == '_';
}
private static boolean isLetterOrDigit(char c) {
  return isLetter(c) || (c >= '0' && c <= '9');
}
```

2. Change all calls to `Character.isLetter()` to call the static method `isLetter()`. Similarly, change calls to `Character.isLetterOrDigit()` to `isLetterOrDigit()`.

The `gd.xml.XMLReader` class also requires some modifications. Replace the `setEncoding()` method with the following:

```
public void setEncoding(String enc) throws UnsupportedEncodingException {
  if (enc==null) throw new UnsupportedEncodingException();
  else if (enc.equals("ASCII")) enc = ASCII;
  else if (enc.equals("UTF-16")) enc = UTF16B;
  else if (enc.equals("UTF-16BE")) enc = UTF16B;
  else if (enc.equals("UTF-8")) enc = UTF8;
  if (enc!=ASCII && enc!=UTF16B && enc!=UTF16L && enc!=UTF8)
    throw new UnsupportedEncodingException();
  encoding = enc;
}
```

Finally, in the `gd.xml.tiny.TinyParser` class, remove references to `java.net.URL` as follows:

1. Comment out the `import java.net.*` line.

2. Comment out the `parseXML(URL url)` method.

3. Comment out the `parseXML(String fname)` method.

When that is done, TinyXML will build in a MIDP environment. (Christian Sauer followed a similar process to port TinyXML to the CLDC PalmOS implementation. Details are here: http://www.kvmworld.com/Articles/TinyXML.shtml.)

To use TinyXML, create an instance of gd.xml.tiny.TinyParser and call its parseXML() method, as follows:

```
String filename = "example1.xml";
InputStream rawIn = this.getClass().getResourceAsStream(filename);
Reader in = new InputStreamReader(rawIn);
try {
  TinyParser p = new TinyParser();
  ParsedXML root = p.parseXML(rawIn);
}
catch (Exception e) { // Handle exceptions. }
```

The parseXML() method returns an instance of ParsedXML representing the root of the document. You can browse the elements of the document by calling ParsedXML methods like getName(), getContent(), attributes(), and elements().

Note that TinyXML is picky about its supported encoding types. The supported encoding types are "ASCII," "UTF-16," "UTF-16BE," and "UTF-8." If the encoding specified in the "<?xml ... ?>" tag of your document does not match one of these types, the parser will throw an exception and quit.

SWX

SWX is an interesting piece of software, a SAX 1.0 parser that reads WAP Binary XML (WBXML). WBXML is a binary encoding of XML that is designed to reduce the size of XML documents. (See http://www.w3.org/TR/wbxml/ for more information.) If you're worried about data transmission times (as you may well be), you might consider encoding your XML at the server side to WBXML and using this parser on the client side.

Like some of the other parsers we've looked at, SWX needs some modifications before it will build in a MIDP environment. First, you will need to supply a dummy java.util.Locale class. If you're using the J2MEWTK, save the following in *<J2MEWTK>/apps/<projectname>/src/java/util*.

```
package java.util;
public class Locale {
}
```

In the `org.xml.sax.helpers.ParserFactory` class, replace the body of the no-argument `makeParser()` method with the following:

```
String className = DEFAULT_PARSER;
return makeParser(className);
```

Finally, the `convert()` method in `de.trantor.wap.WbxmlEncoder` uses the `writeTo()` method of `ByteArrayOutputStream`, which is not defined in the MIDP environment. This is easy enough to fix. In the `convert()` method, find the following code:

```
stringTableBuf.writeTo (out);
buf.writeTo (out);
```

Change the two calls as follows:

```
out.write(stringTableBuf.toByteArray());
out.write(buf.toByteArray());
```

With these changes, SWX will build in a MIDP environment.

To actually use the parser, create an instance of `de.trantor.wap.WbxmlParser` and use it pretty much as you would a regular SAX 1.0 parser. For full SAX compatibility, a `SAXWrapper` class is provided. Basic parsing code looks a lot like any other SAX 1.0 parsing code:

```
WbxmlParser p = new WbxmlParser();
// Set up a DocumentHandler named handler.
p.setDocumentHandler(handler);
p.parse(rawIn);
```

> **NOTE** *The SWX package includes a utility class,* `WbxmlEncoder`, *which converts regular XML to WBXML. It's a little rough around the edges but can be used to convert XML documents to WBXML for testing.* `WbxmlEncoder` *itself depends on the* `com.sun.xml.parser.Parser` *class, which you may or may not have lying around on your system. I found it in my copy of Tomcat 3.1, in the* `lib/xml.jar` *file.*

Summary

The world of XML on small devices is wild and untamed. Bold developers can parse XML in a MIDP environment using one of the five parsers described in this chapter. As a means of transmitting data from server to client, XML is a great choice. Just remember to keep those documents small and simple.

CHAPTER 12

Protecting Network Data

MIDlets are undeniably cool—Java code that runs on a small device, and HTTP network connectivity, as well. But once you start thinking about the possibilities, you realize that a lot of applications just aren't possible without some form of data security. What if you were going to buy something? You shouldn't send credit card numbers over the Internet without some kind of protection. You shouldn't be sending sensitive corporate information over the Internet to small devices. Many applications, then, need something else—something that keeps sensitive data from being stolen. The answer in the MIDP world is no different than the answer anywhere else: cryptography.

Cryptography Review

Cryptography is a branch of mathematics. It's based on the idea that certain kinds of mathematical problems are hard to solve. Using cryptography is a bit speculative; as research in mathematics continues, it's very possible that someone will discover a way to solve (or "break") most of the modern cryptographic algorithms. Nevertheless, for today at least, cryptography provides protection for sensitive data, and there aren't many acceptable alternatives in the everything-connects-to-everything modern world.

The Internet Is a Big Room

There are many aspects to the security of a system. We'll focus on the data your MIDlet sends and receives over the network. This data travels over some infrastructure we know nothing about (provided by your mobile carrier) and probably over the Internet, as well. The Internet is not a secure network, for sure, and your carrier's mobile infrastructure probably isn't either. If you're passing sensitive data around, it's very possible that eavesdroppers at various points in the network can listen in on the data. They may even be able to change parts of it. If your MIDP application involves passing around credit card numbers or sensitive corporate data, you should be concerned.

Think of the Internet as a big room. You can talk to anyone else in the room, but everyone else can listen in on the conversation. Furthermore, you may be talking to someone on the other side of the room through intermediaries, like the children's game of "telephone." Any one of the intermediaries might be changing the conversation, and they can all hear what you're saying.

Data Security Needs and Cryptographic Solutions

Your applications will have some or all of the following data security needs:

- *Integrity*. At the simplest level, you'd like to be sure that the data you're sending is not getting changed or corrupted in any way. This is data integrity.

- *Authentication*. It's often important to verify the identity of the machine or person on the other end of your network connection. Authentication is the process of proving identity.

- *Confidentiality*. If you're sending sensitive data over the network, other people shouldn't be able to see that information. This is confidentiality.

Cryptography provides solutions for each of these needs:

- *Message digests*. A message digest smushes a large piece of data into a small piece of data. You might, for example, run an entire file through a message digest to end up with a 160-bit digest value. If you change even 1 bit of the file and run it through the message digest again, you'll get an entirely different digest value. A message digest value is sometimes called a *digital fingerprint*.

- *Digital signatures*. A digital signature is like a message digest except it is produced by a particular person, the *signer*. The signer must have a *private key* that is used to create the signature. A corresponding *public key* can be used by anyone to verify that the signature came from the signer. The private key and public key together are called a *key pair*. Keys are really just data—think of an array of bytes. *Certificates* are really just an extension of digital signatures. A certificate is a document, signed by some authority like the U.S. Postal Service, that proves your identity. It's like a driver's license, except it's based on digital signatures.

- *Ciphers*. Ciphers can either encrypt data or decrypt it. An encrypting cipher accepts your data, called *plaintext*, and produces an unreadable mess, called *ciphertext*. A decrypting cipher takes ciphertext and converts it back to plaintext. Ciphers use keys; if you encrypt the same plaintext with two different keys, you'll get two different sets of ciphertext. A *symmetric* cipher uses the same key for encryption and decryption. An *asymmetric* cipher operates with a key pair—one key is used for encrypting, while the matching key is used for decrypting.

Ciphers operate in different *modes* that determine how plaintext is encrypted into ciphertext. This, in turn, affects the use and security of the cipher.

> **NOTE** *For comprehensive coverage of cryptographic concepts and algorithms, see Bruce Schneier's* Applied Cryptography *(Wiley, 1995). To find out more about the JCA and JCE in J2SE, read* Java Cryptography *(O'Reilly, 1998).*

The Bouncy Castle Cryptography Package

In the J2SE world, Sun provides support for cryptography through the Java Cryptography Architecture (JCA) and the Java Cryptography Extension (JCE). The problem, of course, is that the JCA and JCE are too heavy for the MIDP platform. So far, Sun is not providing any solutions for cryptography in J2ME. At JavaOne in 1999, they demonstrated what appeared to be MIDP plus SSL support, but no product has come from it yet. You can read more about it in a few conference session slides available here: `http://playground.sun.com/~vgupta/KSSL/`.

It is probably only a matter of time before someone integrates SSL with a MIDP implementation. After all, the generic connection framework means that an implementation could support *https* connections transparently. Although MIDP requires only HTTP support, implementations are free to support other types of connections.

In the meantime, your best bet is the Bouncy Castle cryptography package, an open source effort based in Australia. It's a wonderful piece of work, featuring a clean API and a formidable toolbox of cryptographic algorithms. There are several other open source cryptography packages around the world, but Bouncy Castle specifically offers a lightweight J2ME distribution of their software. To download the package, go to `http://www.bouncycastle.org/`, follow the link for **latest releases**, and choose the **J2ME** release.

Download the zip file into the location of your choice. If you're using the J2MEWTK, follow these instructions to put the Bouncy Castle classes in your project:

1. Copy the *java* and *org* directories from the *src* directory into the *src* directory of your J2MEWTK project.

2. Remove the *org/bouncycastle/crypto/examples* directory and the *org/bouncycastle/crypto/test* directory.

Now your J2MEWTK project should compile without errors. You can go ahead and write MIDlets that use the Bouncy Castle package.

Protecting Passwords with a Message Digest

Having installed and compiled the Bouncy Castle cryptography package, let's try a simple example involving authentication. Computer systems often use passwords instead of digital signatures (or certificates) because they're so much easier. A password is a *shared secret*, which means that you know it and the server knows it, but nobody else should know it.

The Problem with Passwords

The problem with passwords is that you don't want to send them over an insecure network. Imagine, for example, that your MIDlet requires the user to sign on to a server using a user name and password. On the MID, you key in your user name and password, then click the button to send the information up to the server. Unfortunately, your data is sent as plaintext in some HTTP request. Anybody snooping on the network can easily lift your password.

Using a Message Digest

Message digests provides a way to solve this problem. Instead of sending a password as plaintext, you create a message digest value from the password and send that instead. An attacker could just steal the digest value, of course, so you add some other stuff to the digest as well so that only the server, knowing the password, can recreate the same digest value. Figure 12-1 shows the process.

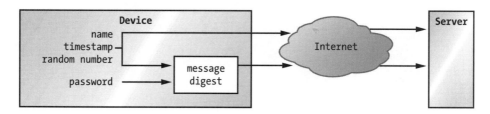

Figure 12-1. Protecting a password with a message digest

The MIDlet creates a timestamp and a random number, both of which are fed into the message digest along with the user name and the password. Then the MIDlet sends the user name, the timestamp, the random number, and the digest value up to the server. It does not send the password as cleartext, but the password is used to calculate the digest value.

The server takes the user name and looks up the corresponding password, which should be stored securely in a file or a database. Then it creates a digest value of the user name, password, timestamp, and random number. If the digest value created on the server matches the digest value sent by the client MIDlet, then the server knows that the user typed in the right password. The user has just logged in successfully.

The server needs some logic to prevent replay attacks. Specifically, the server should reject login attempts that use timestamps and random numbers that have been used before with that login. Although you could save the random numbers and timestamps of all user login attempts, it would be relatively expensive to compare each of these every time a user wanted to login. An easier way to implement this is to save the timestamp of each user's last login attempt. For each subsequent login attempt, the server looks up the saved timestamp. If the timestamp on the current attempt is later than the saved timestamp, the attempt is allowed. The current attempt's timestamp replaces the saved timestamp for this user.

Using the Bouncy Castle Cryptography Package

In the Bouncy Castle package, message digests are generically represented by the org.bouncycastle.crypto.Digest interface. You can add data into the message digest using one of two update() methods. To calculate the message digest value, call doFinal(). Specific implementations of the Digest interface are contained in the org.bouncycastle.crypto.digests package. We'll be using one called SHA1Digest, which implements the SHA-1 digest algorithm. The following line shows how to create a SHA-1 message digest object:

```
Digest digest = new SHA1Digest();
```

The cryptography code is pretty simple. Most of our effort, in fact, is devoted to converting the timestamp and random number to bytes that can be pushed into the message digest object. Then it's just a matter of calling the update() method with each array of bytes.

To calculate the digest, call Digest's doFinal() method. You'll need to pass in a byte array to hold the message digest value. To find out how long this array should be, call the getDigestSize() method.

```
byte[] digestValue = new byte[digest.getDigestSize()];
digest.doFinal(digestValue, 0);
```

Implementing a Protected Password Protocol

This section details an implementation of protected password login. On the client side, a MIDlet collects a user name and password, as shown in Figure 12-2.

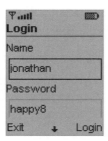

Figure 12-2. A simple form collects a user name and password.

When the **Login** command is invoked, the MIDlet sends data to a servlet, which determines whether or not the client is authenticated. The servlet sends back a message, which is displayed on the screen of the device, as shown in Figure 12-3.

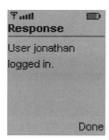

Figure 12-3. The server says whether you're logged in or not.

The MIDlet and servlet exchange various byte arrays, such as the timestamp, the random number, and the message digest value. To make this work smoothly in the context of HTTP headers, which are plain text, the byte arrays are exchanged as hexadecimal strings. A helper class, HexCodec, handles the translation between hexadecimal strings and byte arrays. This same class is used by the MIDlet and the servlet.

Let's look at the MIDlet first. Its main screen is a form where the user can enter a user name and a password. You might be tempted to use a PASSWORD TextField, but I chose not to. For one thing, it's hard to know exactly what text you're entering . For another thing, I'm assuming that the screen of a small device is reasonably private—probably no one will be peeking over your shoulder as you enter your password.

When the user invokes the **Login** command, the MIDlet calculates a message digest value as described above. It assembles various parameters into an HTTP request. It then reads the response from the server and displays the response in an Alert.

The meat of the protected password algorithm is in the login() method. We create a timestamp and a random number and convert these values to byte arrays using a helper method:

```
long timestamp = System.currentTimeMillis();
long randomNumber = mRandom.nextLong();
byte[] timestampBytes = getBytes(timestamp);
byte[] randomBytes = getBytes(randomNumber);
```

The user name and password strings, which come from the MIDlet's main form, are easily converted to byte arrays.

The entire source code for PasswordMIDlet is shown in Listing 12-1.

Listing 12-1. PasswordMIDlet, a protected password client.

```
import java.io.*;
import java.util.Random;

import javax.microedition.io.*;
import javax.microedition.midlet.*;
import javax.microedition.lcdui.*;

import org.bouncycastle.crypto.Digest;
import org.bouncycastle.crypto.digests.SHA1Digest;

public class PasswordMIDlet extends MIDlet {
  private Display mDisplay;
  private Form mForm;
  private TextField mUserField, mPasswordField;
  private Random mRandom;

  public void startApp() {
    mDisplay = Display.getDisplay(this);
    mRandom = new Random(System.currentTimeMillis());

    if (mForm == null) {
      mForm = new Form("Login");
      mUserField = new TextField("Name", "jonathan", 32, 0);
      mPasswordField = new TextField("Password", "happy8", 32, 0);
      mForm.append(mUserField);
      mForm.append(mPasswordField);
```

```
        mForm.addCommand(new Command("Exit", Command.EXIT, 0));
        mForm.addCommand(new Command("Login", Command.SCREEN, 0));
        mForm.setCommandListener(new CommandListener() {
          public void commandAction(Command c, Displayable s) {
            if (c.getCommandType() == Command.EXIT) notifyDestroyed();
            else login();
          }
        });
      }

      mDisplay.setCurrent(mForm);
    }

    private void login() {
      // Gather the values we'll need.
      long timestamp = System.currentTimeMillis();
      long randomNumber = mRandom.nextLong();
      String user = mUserField.getString();
      byte[] userBytes = user.getBytes();
      byte[] timestampBytes = getBytes(timestamp);
      byte[] randomBytes = getBytes(randomNumber);
      String password = mPasswordField.getString();
      byte[] passwordBytes = password.getBytes();

      // Create the message digest.
      Digest digest = new SHA1Digest();
      // Calculate the digest value.
      digest.update(userBytes, 0, userBytes.length);
      digest.update(timestampBytes, 0, timestampBytes.length);
      digest.update(randomBytes, 0, randomBytes.length);
      digest.update(passwordBytes, 0, passwordBytes.length);
      byte[] digestValue = new byte[digest.getDigestSize()];
      digest.doFinal(digestValue, 0);

      // Create the GET URL. The hex encoded message digest value is
      //    included as a parameter.
      URLBuilder ub = new URLBuilder(getAppProperty("PasswordMIDlet.baseURL"));
      ub.addParameter("user", user);
      ub.addParameter("timestamp",
          new String(HexCodec.bytesToHex(timestampBytes)));
      ub.addParameter("random",
          new String(HexCodec.bytesToHex(randomBytes)));
      ub.addParameter("digest",
          new String(HexCodec.bytesToHex(digestValue)));
      String url = ub.toString();
```

```
    try {
      // Query the server and retrieve the response.
      HttpConnection hc = (HttpConnection)Connector.open(url);
      InputStream in = hc.openInputStream();

      int length = (int)hc.getLength();
      byte[] raw = new byte[length];
      in.read(raw);
      String response = new String(raw);
      Alert a = new Alert("Response", response, null, null);
      a.setTimeout(Alert.FOREVER);
      mDisplay.setCurrent(a, mForm);
      in.close();
      hc.close();
    }
    catch (IOException ioe) {
      Alert a = new Alert("Exception", ioe.toString(), null, null);
      a.setTimeout(Alert.FOREVER);
      mDisplay.setCurrent(a, mForm);
    }
  }

  private byte[] getBytes(long x) {
    byte[] bytes = new byte[8];
    for (int i = 0; i < 8; i++)
      bytes[i] = (byte)(x >> ((7 - i) * 8));
    return bytes;
  }

  public void pauseApp() {}

  public void destroyApp(boolean unconditional) {}
}
```

The HexCodec class contains a few static methods for converting between byte arrays and hex encoded strings. The complete class is shown in Listing 12-2.

Listing 12-2. The HexCodec helper class.

```
public class HexCodec {
  private static final char[] kDigits = {
    '0', '1', '2', '3', '4', '5', '6', '7', '8', '9',
    'a', 'b', 'c', 'd', 'e', 'f'
  };
```

```
public static char[] bytesToHex(byte[] raw) {
  int length = raw.length;
  char[] hex = new char[length * 2];
  for (int i = 0; i < length; i++) {
    int value = (raw[i] + 256) % 256;
    int highIndex = value >> 4;
    int lowIndex = value & 0x0f;
    hex[i * 2 + 0] = kDigits[highIndex];
    hex[i * 2 + 1] = kDigits[lowIndex];
  }
  return hex;
}

public static byte[] hexToBytes(char[] hex) {
  int length = hex.length / 2;
  byte[] raw = new byte[length];
  for (int i = 0; i < length; i++) {
    int high = Character.digit(hex[i * 2], 16);
    int low = Character.digit(hex[i * 2 + 1], 16);
    int value = (high << 4) | low;
    if (value > 127) value -= 256;
    raw[i] = (byte)value;
  }
  return raw;
}

public static byte[] hexToBytes(String hex) {
  return hexToBytes(hex.toCharArray());
}
}
```

PasswordMIDlet also uses the URLBuilder class, which provides a simple interface for assembling GET URLs. The URLBuilder class is shown in Listing 12-3.

Listing 12-3. The URLBuilder helper class.

```
public class URLBuilder {
  private StringBuffer mBuffer;
  private boolean mHasParameters;

  public URLBuilder(String base) {
    mBuffer = new StringBuffer(base);
    mHasParameters = false;
  }
```

```
  public void addParameter(String name, String value) {
    // Append a separator.
    if (mHasParameters == false) {
      mBuffer.append('?');
      mHasParameters = true;
    }
    else
      mBuffer.append('&');
    // Now tack on the name and value pair. These should
    //   really be URL encoded (see java.net.URLEncoder in
    //   J2SE) but this class appends the name and value
    //   as is, for simplicity. Names or values with spaces
    //   or other special characters will not work correctly.
    mBuffer.append(name);
    mBuffer.append('=');
    mBuffer.append(value);
  }

  public String toString() {
    return mBuffer.toString();
  }
}
```

A simple implementation of a protected password servlet is shown in
Listing 12-4.

Listing 12-4. The PasswordServlet class.

```
import javax.servlet.http.*;
import javax.servlet.*;
import java.io.*;
import java.util.*;

import org.bouncycastle.crypto.Digest;
import org.bouncycastle.crypto.digests.SHA1Digest;

public class PasswordServlet extends HttpServlet {
  public void doGet(HttpServletRequest request,
      HttpServletResponse response)
      throws ServletException, IOException {
    System.out.println("user = " + request.getParameter("user"));
    System.out.println("timestamp = " + request.getParameter("timestamp"));
    System.out.println("random = " + request.getParameter("random"));
    System.out.println("digest = " + request.getParameter("digest"));
```

```
        // Retrieve the user name.
        String user = request.getParameter("user");
        // Look up the password for this user.
        String password = lookupPassword(user);
        // Pull the timestamp and random number (hex encoded) out of
        //   of the request.
        String timestamp = request.getParameter("timestamp");
        String randomNumber = request.getParameter("random");

        // Here we would compare the timestamp with the last saved
        //   timestamp for this user. We should only accept timestamps
        //   that are greater than the last saved timestamp for this user.

        // Gather values for the message digest.
        byte[] userBytes = user.getBytes();
        byte[] timestampBytes = HexCodec.hexToBytes(timestamp);
        byte[] randomBytes = HexCodec.hexToBytes(randomNumber);
        byte[] passwordBytes = password.getBytes();
        // Create the message digest.
        Digest digest = new SHA1Digest();
        // Calculate the digest value.
        digest.update(userBytes, 0, userBytes.length);
        digest.update(timestampBytes, 0, timestampBytes.length);
        digest.update(randomBytes, 0, randomBytes.length);
        digest.update(passwordBytes, 0, passwordBytes.length);
        byte[] digestValue = new byte[digest.getDigestSize()];
        digest.doFinal(digestValue, 0);

        // Now compare the digest values.
        String message = "";
        String clientDigest = request.getParameter("digest");
        if (isEqual(digestValue, HexCodec.hexToBytes(clientDigest)))
          message = "User " + user + " logged in.";
        else
          message = "Login was unsuccessful.";

        // Send a response to the client.
        response.setContentType("text/plain");
        response.setContentLength(message.length());
        PrintWriter out = response.getWriter();
        out.println(message);
    }
```

```
private String lookupPassword(String user) {
  // Here we would do a real lookup based on the user name.
  //   We might look in a text file or a database. Here, we
  //   just use a hardcoded value.
  return "happy8";
}

private boolean isEqual(byte[] one, byte[] two) {
  if (one.length != two.length) return false;
  for (int i = 0; i < one.length; i++)
    if (one[i] != two[i]) return false;
  return true;
}
}
```

The basic procedure is to pull the parameters out of the request from the MIDlet, and then independently calculate the message digest value. The servlet looks up the user's password in the lookupPassword() method. In a more serious implementation, the servlet would probably look up the password in a database of some sort.

Once the servlet figures out the user's password, it pumps the user name, password, timestamp, and random number into a message digest. Then it calculates the message digest value and compares this result with the digest value that was sent from the MIDlet. If the digest values match, the MIDlet client is authenticated.

Suggested Enhancements

One obvious enhancement to this system is to actually retrieve passwords (on the server side) from a database or password repository of some sort.

Furthermore, the servlet needs to validate the timestamp it receives from the client. Every time a user tries to login, the servlet should make sure that the user's timestamp is greater than the timestamp from the user's previous login attempt.

One possible enhancement on the client side is to store the user's name and password in a record store so they can be automatically sent with each login attempt. Normally this might seem like a bad idea. But small devices are generally kept physically secure by their owners—you try to keep your mobile phone in your possession at all times, or you lock it up somewhere. It's a trade-off between convenience and security. But just considering how difficult it is to enter text on a mobile phone keypad, you might want to give your users the convenience of using a stored name and password.

Note that the authentication performed in this scheme is *per request*. Each time the client sends an HTTP request to the server, it is an entirely separate conversation. Each time, therefore, the client needs to authenticate itself to the server to perform some work, it must go through the whole process again—creating a timestamp and random number, calculating a message digest, and sending the whole mess up to the server. In this system, then, you would probably add parameters to the HTTP request that specify an action or command that should be performed on behalf of the authenticated user.

Securing Network Data

Let's look at something a little more complicated. Suppose you wish to conceal the data you are sending over the network. The protected password example showed one way for a client to authenticate itself to the server, but we've still got the problem of eavesdroppers picking up credit card numbers or other sensitive information off the network.

This example consists of a matched MIDlet and servlet. The MIDlet, StealthMIDlet, has a simple user interface that allows you to enter a message. This message is encrypted using an RC4 stream cipher and sent to the servlet. On the server side, StealthServlet receives the encrypted message, decrypts it, and sends back its own encrypted message. Both messages pass over the insecure Internet as ciphertext, which is difficult for attackers to read without the proper keys.

RC4 is a symmetric encryption algorithm, which means that the same key is used to encrypt and decrypt data. StealthMIDlet and StealthServlet use two keys, one for each direction of data travel. One key is used to encrypt data in the MIDlet and decrypt it in the servlet; the other key encrypts data in the servlet and decrypts it in the MIDlet.

The servlet services multiple client MIDlets, each with their own encrypting and decrypting keys. Therefore, the servlet must keep track of two keys per client without getting them mixed up. It uses an HTTP session object to do this. Every time a client request is received, the servlet finds the corresponding ciphers in the session object. If the ciphers don't exist, they are created and initialized using client-specific keys.

This system provides both data confidentiality and authentication. The client and server are authenticated to each other because they must possess the correct keys to exchange data.

Figure 12-4 shows the main user interface of StealthMIDlet. It allows you to enter a message you want to encrypt and send to the server. When you're ready, hit the **Send** command to kick things off.

Figure 12-4. Enter your secret message in StealthMIDlet*'s main screen.*

The servlet decrypts your message and sends back an encrypted response, which is displayed by the MIDlet as shown in Figure 12-5.

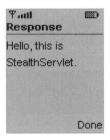

Figure 12-5. The servlet sends back its own secret message.

Using Bouncy Castle Ciphers

In the Bouncy Castle cryptography package, stream ciphers are represented by the org.bouncycastle.crypto.StreamCipher interface. You just need to initialize the cipher, using init(), and then you can encrypt or decrypt data using processBytes().

The Bouncy Castle package only provides one direct stream cipher implementation, org.bouncycastle.crypto.engines.RC4. If you'd prefer to use a different algorithm, you can use a block cipher instead. You can treat block ciphers like stream ciphers using Cipher Feedback (CFB) mode. In the Bouncy Castle package, this is implemented in the org.bouncycastle.crypto.StreamBlockCipher class. This technique gives you access to Bouncy Castle's considerable arsenal of block cipher implementations, from the wizened DES through Blowfish, Rijndael, and more. For more information on cipher modes, see Chapter 7 of *Java Cryptography*.

Our simple implementation instantiates a couple of RC4 objects, something like this:

```
StreamCipher inCipher = new RC4Engine();
StreamCipher outCipher = new RC4Engine();
```

The ciphers need to be initialized before they can be used. The first parameter to init() should be true if the cipher will be encrypting data, false for decryption. The second parameter is essentially the key, wrapped up in a KeyParameter object.

```
// Assume we have retrieved inKey and outKey, both byte arrays.
inCipher.init(false, new KeyParameter(inKey));
outCipher.init(true, new KeyParameter(outKey));
```

To encrypt data, we just need to create an array to hold the ciphertext. Then call the stream cipher's processBytes() method to perform the encryption. The processBytes() method accepts the plaintext array, an index into the plaintext, the number of bytes that should be processed, the ciphertext array, and the index at which the ciphertext should be written.

```
// Assume we have a byte array called plaintext.
byte[] ciphertext = new byte[plaintext.length];
outCipher.processBytes(plaintext, 0, plaintext.length, ciphertext, 0);
```

Decryption is identical, except you would use a cipher that has been initialized for decryption.

Implementation

The source code for StealthMIDlet is shown in Listing 12-5. This MIDlet has a simple user interface, initialized in the startApp() method. The MIDlet's ciphers are also created and initialized in startApp().

Listing 12-5. StealthMIDlet, a data encryption MIDlet.

```
import java.io.*;

import javax.microedition.io.*;
import javax.microedition.midlet.*;
import javax.microedition.lcdui.*;
```

```
import org.bouncycastle.crypto.StreamCipher;
import org.bouncycastle.crypto.engines.RC4Engine;
import org.bouncycastle.crypto.params.KeyParameter;

public class StealthMIDlet extends MIDlet {
  private Display mDisplay;
  private TextBox mTextBox;

  private String mSession;
  private StreamCipher mOutCipher, mInCipher;

  public StealthMIDlet() {
    mOutCipher = new RC4Engine();
    mInCipher = new RC4Engine();
  }

  public void startApp() {
    if (mSession == null) {
      // Load the keys from resource files.
      byte[] inKey = getInKey();
      byte[] outKey = getOutKey();

      // Initialize the ciphers.
      mOutCipher.init(true, new KeyParameter(outKey));
      mInCipher.init(false, new KeyParameter(inKey));
    }

    mDisplay = Display.getDisplay(this);

    if (mTextBox == null) {
      mTextBox = new TextBox("StealthMIDlet", "The eagle has landed", 256, 0);

      mTextBox.addCommand(new Command("Exit", Command.EXIT, 0));
      mTextBox.addCommand(new Command("Send", Command.SCREEN, 0));
      mTextBox.setCommandListener(new CommandListener() {
        public void commandAction(Command c, Displayable s) {
          if (c.getCommandType() == Command.EXIT) notifyDestroyed();
          else send();
        }
      });
    }

    mDisplay.setCurrent(mTextBox);
  }
```

```
private void send() {
  // Encrypt our message.
  byte[] plaintext = mTextBox.getString().getBytes();
  byte[] ciphertext = new byte[plaintext.length];
  mOutCipher.processBytes(plaintext, 0, plaintext.length, ciphertext, 0);
  char[] hexCiphertext = HexCodec.bytesToHex(ciphertext);

  // Create the GET URL. Our user name and the encrypted, hex
  //   encoded message are included as parameters. The user name
  //   and base URL are retrieved as application properties.
  String baseURL = getAppProperty("StealthMIDlet.baseURL");
  URLBuilder ub = new URLBuilder(baseURL);
  ub.addParameter("user", getAppProperty("StealthMIDlet.user"));
  ub.addParameter("message", new String(hexCiphertext));
  String url = ub.toString();

  try {
    // Query the server and retrieve the response.
    HttpConnection hc = (HttpConnection)Connector.open(url);
    if (mSession != null)
      hc.setRequestProperty("cookie", mSession);
    InputStream in = hc.openInputStream();

    String cookie = hc.getHeaderField("Set-cookie");
    if (cookie != null) {
      int semicolon = cookie.indexOf(';');
      mSession = cookie.substring(0, semicolon);
    }

    int length = (int)hc.getLength();
    ciphertext = new byte[length];
    in.read(ciphertext);
    in.close();
    hc.close();
  }
  catch (IOException ioe) {
    Alert a = new Alert("Exception", ioe.toString(), null, null);
    a.setTimeout(Alert.FOREVER);
    mDisplay.setCurrent(a, mTextBox);
  }
```

```
    // Decrypt the server response.
    String hex = new String(ciphertext);
    byte[] dehexed = HexCodec.hexToBytes(hex.toCharArray());
    byte[] deciphered = new byte[dehexed.length];
    mInCipher.processBytes(dehexed, 0, dehexed.length, deciphered, 0);

    String decipheredString = new String(deciphered);
    Alert a = new Alert("Response", decipheredString, null, null);
    a.setTimeout(Alert.FOREVER);
    mDisplay.setCurrent(a, mTextBox);
  }


  // Normally you would probably read keys from resource files
  //    in the MIDlet suite JAR, using the getResourceAsStream()
  //    method in Class. Here I just use hardcoded values that match
  //    the hardcoded values in StealthServlet.
  private byte[] getInKey() {
    return "Incoming MIDlet key".getBytes();
  }

  private byte[] getOutKey() {
    return "Outgoing MIDlet key".getBytes();
  }


  public void pauseApp() {}

  public void destroyApp(boolean unconditional) {}
}
```

When the user invokes the **Send** command, StealthMIDlet encrypts the user's message with its outgoing cipher. It then encodes the ciphertext as hexadecimal text in preparation for sending it to the servlet. The user's name and the ciphertext is packaged into a GET URL and sent to the server. Additionally, StealthMIDlet keeps track of a cookie that is used for session tracking. If the server sends back a session id cookie, it is saved in StealthMIDlet's mSession member variable. The saved cookie is sent with each subsequent request. This allows the server to retrieve session information for this client. Without this session information, each HTTP request from client to server would need to reinitialize the ciphers so they didn't get unsynchronized.

StealthMIDlet retrieves the response from the server as hexadecimal ciphertext. It converts the string to a byte array, and then decrypts the byte array using the MIDlet's incoming cipher. The decrypted message is displayed in an Alert.

StealthMIDlet makes use of the same HexCodec and URLBuilder classes that were presented earlier in this chapter.

On the server side, things are a little more complicated. StealthServlet should be capable of handling multiple clients, which means it should maintain a pair of ciphers for each user that connects. This is done using HTTP sessions, one session per user. When a client request comes in, StealthServlet attempts to find two ciphers in the user's session. If they don't exist, as will be the case the first time a user connects to the servlet, new ciphers are created. The ciphers are initialized using keys that are unique to each user. Exactly how these keys are located is left up to you. In this simple implementation, the getInKey() and getOutKey() methods are hard-coded.

You should notice that the keys on the servlet side appear to be reversed from the MIDlet. This is because the servlet's incoming cipher should decrypt using the same key as the MIDlet's outgoing cipher.

Once StealthServlet has located or created the ciphers that correspond to a particular user, it decrypts the incoming message and prints it out to the server console. Then it encrypts a response message (also hard-coded) and sends the response back to the MIDlet.

The entire StealthServlet class is shown in Listing 12-6.

Listing 12-6. The source code for StealthServlet.

```
import javax.servlet.http.*;
import javax.servlet.*;
import java.io.*;
import java.util.*;

import org.bouncycastle.crypto.StreamCipher;
import org.bouncycastle.crypto.engines.RC4Engine;
import org.bouncycastle.crypto.params.KeyParameter;

public class StealthServlet extends HttpServlet {
  public void doGet(HttpServletRequest request,
      HttpServletResponse response)
      throws ServletException, IOException {
    String user = request.getParameter("user");

    // Try to find the user's cipher pair.
    HttpSession session = request.getSession();
    StreamCipher inCipher = (StreamCipher)session.getAttribute("inCipher");
    StreamCipher outCipher = (StreamCipher)session.getAttribute("outCipher");
```

```
  // If the ciphers aren't found, create and initialize a new pair.
  if (inCipher == null && outCipher == null) {
    // Retrieve the client's keys.
    byte[] inKey = getInKey(user);
    byte[] outKey = getOutKey(user);
    // Create and initialize the ciphers.
    inCipher = new RC4Engine();
    outCipher = new RC4Engine();
    inCipher.init(true, new KeyParameter(inKey));
    outCipher.init(false, new KeyParameter(outKey));
    // Now put them in the session object.
    session.setAttribute("inCipher", inCipher);
    session.setAttribute("outCipher", outCipher);
  }

  // Retrieve the client's message.
  String clientHex = request.getParameter("message");
  byte[] clientCiphertext = HexCodec.hexToBytes(clientHex);
  byte[] clientDecrypted = new byte[clientCiphertext.length];
  inCipher.processBytes(clientCiphertext, 0, clientCiphertext.length,
      clientDecrypted, 0);
  System.out.println("message = " + new String(clientDecrypted));

  // Create the response message.
  String message = "Hello, this is StealthServlet.";

  // Encrypt the message.
  byte[] plaintext = message.getBytes();
  byte[] ciphertext = new byte[plaintext.length];
  outCipher.processBytes(plaintext, 0, plaintext.length, ciphertext, 0);
  char[] hexCiphertext = HexCodec.bytesToHex(ciphertext);

  response.setContentType("text/plain");
  response.setContentLength(hexCiphertext.length);
  PrintWriter out = response.getWriter();
  out.println(hexCiphertext);
}

private byte[] getInKey(String user) {
  return "Outgoing MIDlet key".getBytes();
}
```

```
private byte[] getOutKey(String user) {
  return "Incoming MIDlet key".getBytes();
  }
}
```

Suggested Enhancements

A few relatively minor enhancements would make this a serious application. The first area to tackle is key handling. StealthMIDlet should load its keys from resource files in the MIDlet suite JAR rather than using hard-coded values. This is possible using the getResourceAsStream() method in Class.

Likewise, StealthServlet should locate and load keys from a database or some kind of file respository. Something as simple as a standard naming scheme based on user names might be sufficient.

The keys themselves should be larger than the hard-coded samples here—how large is up to you. As long ago as 1996, the U.S. government was fairly sanguine about allowing the export of 40 bit RC4 technology, so you can rest assured that 40 bits is probably way too short. As the key length increases, of course, you may start to have memory or performance problems, particularly in a constrained environment like MIDP. Try to find a good balance between performance and security.

Furthermore, you might want to consider using a different algorithm, like Blowfish or Rijndael. The Bouncy Castle cryptography package has plenty of options in the org.bouncycastle.crypto.engines package. As I mentioned, you can treat a block cipher like a stream cipher using CFB mode.

Finally, the communication between the servlet and the MIDlet could be improved. It would be nice, for example, if the servlet had some way to tell the MIDlet it couldn't find a session. It's possible that the MIDlet will send up a cookie for a session that has expired on the server side. In the current implementation, the servlet will create a new set of ciphers, ones that are not synchronized with the MIDlet's ciphers. One way to solve this problem would be to have the servlet pass a response code to the MIDlet. One response code might mean, "I lost your session. Please reinitialize your ciphers and try again."

Deployment Issues

Suppose you dressed up this example and incorporated it into a product. What are the issues with distribution? For each copy of your software, you need to generate a pair of keys. These keys are stored as resource files inside the MIDlet suite JAR, which means that for each copy of your software, you'll need to generate a unique MIDlet suite JAR. At the same time, you need to save the keys on the server side somewhere. When the client MIDlet makes a connection, you need to be able to find the corresponding keys. None of this is particularly difficult, and it can be automated.

The MIDlet suite JAR contains keys that should be secret. Therefore, it is a security risk to transmit the JAR to a customer over the Internet. You might transfer it via HTTPS to a customer's browser, and then rely on him or her to install the MIDlet suite on a mobile telephone or other small device via a serial cable.

Trimming Bouncy Castle Down to Size

With both of the examples in this chapter, we're only using a small subset of the Bouncy Castle cryptography package. Since we have the whole source code available, we can take out pieces of the package we don't need in order to save space in the MIDlet suite JAR.

By simply removing whole directories of classes I didn't need, I was able to trim the size of the MIDlet suite for `PasswordMIDlet` and `StealthMIDlet` from 280KB to 114KB. Further trimming is also possible; I just chopped off the large pieces—directories like *org/bouncycastle/asn1* and *org/bouncycastle/crypto/test*. If you remove individual classes and interfaces, further size reductions are possible.

> **NOTE:** *If you try this technique in J2MEWTK, make sure you also remove the* classes *and* tmpclasses *directories in your project directory. Even though you remove a source file, the compiled class file may still be present in* classes *or* tmpclasses. *Removing these directories forces J2MEWTK to recompile everything.*

Summary

Data security is crucial for some types of applications. Data security is feasible in the MIDP world using the Bouncy Castle cryptography package. The Bouncy Castle package provides sophisticated, accessible, industrial-strength cryptography for the MIDP platform. This example presented two possible applications—one using a message digest for secure password authentication, and the other using ciphers to encrypt data sent between a MIDlet and a servlet.

Keep in mind that adding cryptography to an application or system won't necessarily make it more secure. You need to take a comprehensive system-level approach to security. Cryptography is just one of the tools in your box.

MIDP API Reference

This appendix is a reference for the classes and interfaces of the MIDP API. This reference is designed to help you quickly find the signature of a method in the MIDP API. Exceptions and errors are not included.

For a full description of any class, interface, or method, consult the API documentation, either in HTML (usually distributed with a MIDP toolkit) or in the MIDP specification itself.

The API listings are alphabetical, grouped by package.

Package java.io

Class java.io.ByteArrayInputStream

```
public class ByteArrayInputStream
    extends java.io.InputStream {
  // Constructors
  public ByteArrayInputStream(byte[] buf);
  public ByteArrayInputStream(byte[] buf, int offset, int length);

  // Methods
  public synchronized int available();
  public synchronized void close();
  public void mark(int readAheadLimit);
  public boolean markSupported();
  public synchronized int read();
  public synchronized int read(byte[] b, int off, int len);
  public synchronized void reset();
  public synchronized long skip(long n);
}
```

Class java.io.ByteArrayOutputStream

```
public class ByteArrayOutputStream
    extends java.io.OutputStream {
  // Constructors
  public ByteArrayOutputStream();
  public ByteArrayOutputStream(int size);

  // Methods
  public synchronized void close();
  public synchronized void reset();
  public int size();
  public synchronized byte[] toByteArray();
  public synchronized void write(int b);
  public synchronized void write(byte[] b, int off, int len);
}
```

Interface java.io.DataInput

```
public interface DataInput {
  // Methods
  public boolean readBoolean();
  public byte readByte();
  public char readChar();
  public void readFully(byte[] b);
  public void readFully(byte[] b, int off, int len);
  public int readInt();
  public long readLong();
  public short readShort();
  public String readUTF();
  public int readUnsignedByte();
  public int readUnsignedShort();
  public int skipBytes(int n);
}
```

Class java.io.DataInputStream

```
public class DataInputStream
    extends java.io.InputStream
    implements DataInput {
  // Static methods
  public static final String readUTF(DataInput in);
```

```
  // Constructors
  public DataInputStream(InputStream in);

  // Methods
  public int available();
  public void close();
  public synchronized void mark(int readlimit);
  public boolean markSupported();
  public int read();
  public final int read(byte[] b);
  public final int read(byte[] b, int off, int len);
  public final boolean readBoolean();
  public final byte readByte();
  public final char readChar();
  public final void readFully(byte[] b);
  public final void readFully(byte[] b, int off, int len);
  public final int readInt();
  public final long readLong();
  public final short readShort();
  public final String readUTF();
  public final int readUnsignedByte();
  public final int readUnsignedShort();
  public synchronized void reset();
  public long skip(long n);
  public final int skipBytes(int n);
}
```

Interface java.io.DataOutput

```
public interface DataOutput {
  // Methods
  public void write(int b);
  public void write(byte[] b);
  public void write(byte[] b, int off, int len);
  public void writeBoolean(boolean v);
  public void writeByte(int v);
  public void writeChar(int v);
  public void writeChars(String s);
  public void writeInt(int v);
  public void writeLong(long v);
  public void writeShort(int v);
  public void writeUTF(String str);
}
```

Class java.io.DataOutputStream

```
public class DataOutputStream
    extends java.io.OutputStream
    implements DataOutput {
  // Constructors
  public DataOutputStream(OutputStream out);

  // Methods
  public void close();
  public void flush();
  public void write(int b);
  public void write(byte[] b, int off, int len);
  public final void writeBoolean(boolean v);
  public final void writeByte(int v);
  public final void writeChar(int v);
  public final void writeChars(String s);
  public final void writeInt(int v);
  public final void writeLong(long v);
  public final void writeShort(int v);
  public final void writeUTF(String str);
}
```

Class java.io.InputStream

```
public abstract class InputStream {
  // Constructors
  public InputStream();

  // Methods
  public int available();
  public void close();
  public synchronized void mark(int readlimit);
  public boolean markSupported();

  public abstract int read();
  public int read(byte[] b);
  public int read(byte[] b, int off, int len);
  public synchronized void reset();
  public long skip(long n);
}
```

Class java.io.InputStreamReader

```
public class InputStreamReader
    extends java.io.Reader {
  // Constructors
  public InputStreamReader(InputStream is);
  public InputStreamReader(InputStream is, String enc);

  // Methods
  public void close();
  public void mark(int readAheadLimit);
  public boolean markSupported();
  public int read();
  public int read(char[] cbuf, int off, int len);
  public boolean ready();
  public void reset();
  public long skip(long n);
}
```

Class java.io.OutputStream

```
public abstract class OutputStream {
  // Constructors
  public OutputStream();

  // Methods
  public void close();
  public void flush();

  public abstract void write(int b);
  public void write(byte[] b);
  public void write(byte[] b, int off, int len);
}
```

Class java.io.OutputStreamWriter

```
public class OutputStreamWriter
    extends java.io.Writer {
  // Constructors
  public OutputStreamWriter(OutputStream os);
  public OutputStreamWriter(OutputStream os, String enc);
```

```
  // Methods
  public void close();
  public void flush();
  public void write(int c);
  public void write(char[] cbuf, int off, int len);
  public void write(String str, int off, int len);
}
```

Class java.io.PrintStream

```
public class PrintStream
    extends java.io.OutputStream {
  // Constructors
  public PrintStream(OutputStream out);

  // Methods
  public boolean checkError();
  public void close();
  public void flush();
  public void print(boolean b);
  public void print(char c);
  public void print(int i);
  public void print(long l);
  public void print(char[] s);
  public void print(String s);
  public void print(Object obj);
  public void println();
  public void println(boolean x);
  public void println(char x);
  public void println(int x);
  public void println(long x);
  public void println(char[] x);
  public void println(String x);
  public void println(Object x);
  protected void setError();
  public void write(int b);
  public void write(byte[] buf, int off, int len);
}
```

Class java.io.Reader

```
public abstract class Reader {
  // Constructors
  protected Reader();
  protected Reader(Object lock);

  // Methods

  public abstract void close();
  public void mark(int readAheadLimit);
  public boolean markSupported();
  public int read();
  public int read(char[] cbuf);

  public abstract int read(char[] cbuf, int off, int len);
  public boolean ready();
  public void reset();
  public long skip(long n);
}
```

Class java.io.Writer

```
public abstract class Writer {
  // Constructors
  protected Writer();
  protected Writer(Object lock);

  // Methods

  public abstract void close();

  public abstract void flush();
  public void write(int c);
  public void write(char[] cbuf);

  public abstract void write(char[] cbuf, int off, int len);
  public void write(String str);
  public void write(String str, int off, int len);
}
```

Package java.lang

Class java.lang.Boolean

```
public final class Boolean {
  // Constructors
  public Boolean(boolean value);

  // Methods
  public boolean booleanValue();
  public boolean equals(Object obj);
  public int hashCode();
  public String toString();
}
```

Class java.lang.Byte

```
public final class Byte {
  // Constants
  public static final byte MAX_VALUE;
  public static final byte MIN_VALUE;

  // Static methods
  public static byte parseByte(String s);
  public static byte parseByte(String s, int radix);

  // Constructors
  public Byte(byte value);

  // Methods
  public byte byteValue();
  public boolean equals(Object obj);
  public int hashCode();
  public String toString();
}
```

Class java.lang.Character

```
public final class Character {
  // Constants
  public static final int MAX_RADIX;
  public static final char MAX_VALUE;
  public static final int MIN_RADIX;
  public static final char MIN_VALUE;

  // Static methods
  public static int digit(char ch, int radix);
  public static boolean isDigit(char ch);
  public static boolean isLowerCase(char ch);
  public static boolean isUpperCase(char ch);
  public static char toLowerCase(char ch);
  public static char toUpperCase(char ch);

  // Constructors
  public Character(char value);

  // Methods
  public char charValue();
  public boolean equals(Object obj);
  public int hashCode();
  public String toString();
}
```

Class java.lang.Class

```
public final class Class {
  // Static methods
  public static native Class forName(String className);

  // Methods
  public native String getName();
  public InputStream getResourceAsStream(String name);
  public native boolean isArray();
  public native boolean isAssignableFrom(Class cls);
  public native boolean isInstance(Object obj);
  public native boolean isInterface();
  public native Object newInstance();
  public String toString();
}
```

Class java.lang.Integer

```
public final class Integer {
  // Constants
  public static final int MAX_VALUE;
  public static final int MIN_VALUE;

  // Static methods
  public static int parseInt(String s, int radix);
  public static int parseInt(String s);
  public static String toBinaryString(int i);
  public static String toHexString(int i);
  public static String toOctalString(int i);
  public static String toString(int i, int radix);
  public static String toString(int i);
  public static Integer valueOf(String s, int radix);
  public static Integer valueOf(String s);

  // Constructors
  public Integer(int value);

  // Methods
  public byte byteValue();
  public boolean equals(Object obj);
  public int hashCode();
  public int intValue();
  public long longValue();
  public short shortValue();
  public String toString();
}
```

Class java.lang.Long

```
public final class Long {
  // Constants
  public static final long MAX_VALUE;
  public static final long MIN_VALUE;

  // Static methods
  public static long parseLong(String s, int radix);
  public static long parseLong(String s);
  public static String toString(long i, int radix);
  public static String toString(long i);
```

```
  // Constructors
  public Long(long value);

  // Methods
  public boolean equals(Object obj);
  public int hashCode();
  public long longValue();
  public String toString();
}
```

Class java.lang.Math

```
public final class Math {
  // Static methods
  public static int abs(int a);
  public static long abs(long a);
  public static int max(int a, int b);
  public static long max(long a, long b);
  public static int min(int a, int b);
  public static long min(long a, long b);
}
```

Class java.lang.Object

```
public class Object {
  // Constructors
  public Object();

  // Methods
  public boolean equals(Object obj);
  public final native Class getClass();
  public native int hashCode();
  public final native void notify();
  public final native void notifyAll();
  public String toString();
  public final native void wait(long timeout);
  public final void wait(long timeout, int nanos);
  public final void wait();
}
```

Interface java.lang.Runnable

```
public interface Runnable {
  // Methods
  public void run();
}
```

Class java.lang.Runtime

```
public class Runtime {
  // Static methods
  public static Runtime getRuntime();

  // Methods
  public void exit(int status);
  public native long freeMemory();
  public native void gc();
  public native long totalMemory();
}
```

Class java.lang.Short

```
public final class Short {
  // Constants
  public static final short MAX_VALUE;
  public static final short MIN_VALUE;

  // Static methods
  public static short parseShort(String s);
  public static short parseShort(String s, int radix);

  // Constructors
  public Short(short value);

  // Methods
  public boolean equals(Object obj);
  public int hashCode();
  public short shortValue();
  public String toString();
}
```

Class java.lang.String

```
public final class String {
  // Static methods
  public static String valueOf(Object obj);
  public static String valueOf(char[] data);
  public static String valueOf(char[] data, int offset, int count);
  public static String valueOf(boolean b);
  public static String valueOf(char c);
  public static String valueOf(int i);
  public static String valueOf(long l);

  // Constructors
  public String();
  public String(String value);
  public String(char[] value);
  public String(char[] value, int offset, int count);
  public String(byte[] bytes, int off, int len, String enc);
  public String(byte[] bytes, String enc);
  public String(byte[] bytes, int off, int len);
  public String(byte[] bytes);
  public String(StringBuffer buffer);

  // Methods
  public char charAt(int index);
  public int compareTo(String anotherString);
  public String concat(String str);
  public boolean endsWith(String suffix);
  public boolean equals(Object anObject);
  public byte[] getBytes(String enc);
  public byte[] getBytes();
  public void getChars(int srcBegin, int srcEnd, char[] dst,
      int dstBegin);
  public int hashCode();
  public int indexOf(int ch);
  public int indexOf(int ch, int fromIndex);
  public int indexOf(String str);
  public int indexOf(String str, int fromIndex);
  public int lastIndexOf(int ch);
  public int lastIndexOf(int ch, int fromIndex);
  public int length();
  public boolean regionMatches(boolean ignoreCase, int toffset,
      String other, int ooffset, int len);
```

```
      public String replace(char oldChar, char newChar);
      public boolean startsWith(String prefix, int toffset);
      public boolean startsWith(String prefix);
      public String substring(int beginIndex);
      public String substring(int beginIndex, int endIndex);
      public char[] toCharArray();
      public String toLowerCase();
      public String toString();
      public String toUpperCase();
      public String trim();
}
```

Class java.lang.StringBuffer

```
public final class StringBuffer {
  // Constructors
  public StringBuffer();
  public StringBuffer(int length);
  public StringBuffer(String str);

  // Methods
  public synchronized StringBuffer append(Object obj);
  public synchronized StringBuffer append(String str);
  public synchronized StringBuffer append(char[] str);
  public synchronized StringBuffer append(char[] str, int offset,
      int len);
  public StringBuffer append(boolean b);
  public synchronized StringBuffer append(char c);
  public StringBuffer append(int i);
  public StringBuffer append(long l);
  public int capacity();
  public synchronized char charAt(int index);
  public synchronized StringBuffer delete(int start, int end);
  public synchronized StringBuffer deleteCharAt(int index);
  public synchronized void ensureCapacity(int minimumCapacity);
  public synchronized void getChars(int srcBegin, int srcEnd,
      char[] dst, int dstBegin);
  public synchronized StringBuffer insert(int offset, Object obj);
  public synchronized StringBuffer insert(int offset, String str);
  public synchronized StringBuffer insert(int offset, char[] str);
  public StringBuffer insert(int offset, boolean b);
  public synchronized StringBuffer insert(int offset, char c);
  public StringBuffer insert(int offset, int i);
```

```
  public StringBuffer insert(int offset, long l);
  public int length();
  public synchronized StringBuffer reverse();
  public synchronized void setCharAt(int index, char ch);
  public synchronized void setLength(int newLength);
  public String toString();
}
```

Class java.lang.System

```
public final class System {
  // Constants
  public static final PrintStream err;
  public static final PrintStream out;

  // Static methods
  public static native void arraycopy(Object src, int src_position,
      Object dst, int dst_position, int length);
  public static native long currentTimeMillis();
  public static void exit(int status);
  public static void gc();
  public static String getProperty(String key);
  public static native int identityHashCode(Object x);
}
```

Class java.lang.Thread

```
public class Thread
    implements Runnable {
  // Constants
  public static final int MAX_PRIORITY;
  public static final int MIN_PRIORITY;
  public static final int NORM_PRIORITY;

  // Static methods
  public static native int activeCount();
  public static native Thread currentThread();
  public static native void sleep(long millis);
  public static native void yield();

  // Constructors
  public Thread();
  public Thread(Runnable target);
```

```
  // Methods
  public final int getPriority();
  public final native boolean isAlive();
  public final void join();
  public void run();
  public final void setPriority(int newPriority);
  public native synchronized void start();
  public String toString();
}
```

Class java.lang.Throwable

```
public class Throwable {
  // Constructors
  public Throwable();
  public Throwable(String message);

  // Methods
  public String getMessage();
  public void printStackTrace();
  public String toString();
}
```

Package java.util

Class java.util.Calendar

```
public abstract class Calendar {
  // Constants
  public static final int AM;
  public static final int AM_PM;
  public static final int APRIL;
  public static final int AUGUST;
  public static final int DATE;
  public static final int DAY_OF_MONTH;
  public static final int DAY_OF_WEEK;
  public static final int DECEMBER;
  public static final int FEBRUARY;
  public static final int FRIDAY;
  public static final int HOUR;
  public static final int HOUR_OF_DAY;
  public static final int JANUARY;
  public static final int JULY;
  public static final int JUNE;
```

```
  public static final int MARCH;
  public static final int MAY;
  public static final int MILLISECOND;
  public static final int MINUTE;
  public static final int MONDAY;
  public static final int MONTH;
  public static final int NOVEMBER;
  public static final int OCTOBER;
  public static final int PM;
  public static final int SATURDAY;
  public static final int SECOND;
  public static final int SEPTEMBER;
  public static final int SUNDAY;
  public static final int THURSDAY;
  public static final int TUESDAY;
  public static final int WEDNESDAY;
  public static final int YEAR;

  // Static methods
  public static synchronized Calendar getInstance();
  public static synchronized Calendar getInstance(TimeZone zone);

  // Constructors
  protected Calendar();

  // Methods
  public boolean after(Object when);
  public boolean before(Object when);
  public boolean equals(Object obj);
  public final int get(int field);
  public final Date getTime();
  protected long getTimeInMillis();
  public TimeZone getTimeZone();
  public final void set(int field, int value);
  public final void setTime(Date date);
  protected void setTimeInMillis(long millis);
  public void setTimeZone(TimeZone value);
}
```

Class java.util.Date

```
public class Date {
  // Constructors
  public Date();
  public Date(long date);
```

```java
  // Methods
  public boolean equals(Object obj);
  public long getTime();
  public int hashCode();
  public void setTime(long time);
}
```

Interface java.util.Enumeration

```java
public interface Enumeration {
  // Methods
  public boolean hasMoreElements();
  public Object nextElement();
}
```

Class java.util.Hashtable

```java
public class Hashtable {
  // Constructors
  public Hashtable(int initialCapacity);
  public Hashtable();

  // Methods
  public synchronized void clear();
  public synchronized boolean contains(Object value);
  public synchronized boolean containsKey(Object key);
  public synchronized Enumeration elements();
  public synchronized Object get(Object key);
  public boolean isEmpty();
  public synchronized Enumeration keys();
  public synchronized Object put(Object key, Object value);
  protected void rehash();
  public synchronized Object remove(Object key);
  public int size();
  public synchronized String toString();
}
```

Class java.util.Random

```java
public class Random {
  // Constructors
  public Random();
  public Random(long seed);
```

```
  // Methods
  protected synchronized int next(int bits);
  public int nextInt();
  public long nextLong();
  public synchronized void setSeed(long seed);
}
```

Class java.util.Stack

```
public class Stack
    extends java.util.Vector {
  // Constructors
  public Stack();

  // Methods
  public boolean empty();
  public synchronized Object peek();
  public synchronized Object pop();
  public Object push(Object item);
  public synchronized int search(Object o);
}
```

Class java.util.Timer

```
public class Timer {
  // Constructors
  public Timer();

  // Methods
  public void cancel();
  public void schedule(TimerTask task, long delay);
  public void schedule(TimerTask task, Date time);
  public void schedule(TimerTask task, long delay, long period);
  public void schedule(TimerTask task, Date firstTime, long period);
  public void scheduleAtFixedRate(TimerTask task, long delay,
      long period);
  public void scheduleAtFixedRate(TimerTask task, Date firstTime,
      long period);
}
```

Class java.util.TimerTask

```
public abstract class TimerTask
    implements Runnable {
  // Constructors
  protected TimerTask();

  // Methods
  public boolean cancel();

  public abstract void run();
  public long scheduledExecutionTime();
}
```

Class java.util.TimeZone

```
public abstract class TimeZone {
  // Static methods
  public static String getAvailableIDs();
  public static synchronized TimeZone getDefault();
  public static synchronized TimeZone getTimeZone(String ID);

  // Constructors
  public TimeZone();

  // Methods
  public String getID();

  public abstract int getOffset(int era, int year, int month,

      int day, int dayOfWeek, int millis);

  public abstract int getRawOffset();

  public abstract boolean useDaylightTime();
}
```

Class java.util.Vector

```
public class Vector {
  // Constructors
  public Vector(int initialCapacity, int capacityIncrement);
  public Vector(int initialCapacity);
  public Vector();
```

```
// Methods
public synchronized void addElement(Object obj);
public int capacity();
public boolean contains(Object elem);
public synchronized void copyInto(Object[] anArray);
public synchronized Object elementAt(int index);
public synchronized Enumeration elements();
public synchronized void ensureCapacity(int minCapacity);
public synchronized Object firstElement();
public int indexOf(Object elem);
public synchronized int indexOf(Object elem, int index);
public synchronized void insertElementAt(Object obj, int index);
public boolean isEmpty();
public synchronized Object lastElement();
public int lastIndexOf(Object elem);
public synchronized int lastIndexOf(Object elem, int index);
public synchronized void removeAllElements();
public synchronized boolean removeElement(Object obj);
public synchronized void removeElementAt(int index);
public synchronized void setElementAt(Object obj, int index);
public synchronized void setSize(int newSize);
public int size();
public synchronized String toString();
public synchronized void trimToSize();
}
```

Package javax.microedition.io

Class javax.microedition.io.Connector

```
public class Connector {
  // Constants
  public static final int READ;
  public static final int READ_WRITE;
  public static final int WRITE;

  // Static methods
  public static Connection open(String name);
  public static Connection open(String name, int mode);
  public static Connection open(String name, int mode,
      boolean timeouts);
  public static DataInputStream openDataInputStream(String name);
  public static DataOutputStream openDataOutputStream(String name);
  public static InputStream openInputStream(String name);
  public static OutputStream openOutputStream(String name);
}
```

Interface javax.microedition.io.Connection

```
public interface Connection {
  // Methods
  public void close();
}
```

Interface javax.microedition.io.ContentConnection

```
public interface ContentConnection
    implements StreamConnection {
  // Methods
  public String getEncoding();
  public long getLength();
  public String getType();
}
```

Interface javax.microedition.io.Datagram

```
public interface Datagram
    implements DataInput, DataOutput {
  // Methods
  public String getAddress();
  public byte[] getData();
  public int getLength();
  public int getOffset();
  public void reset();
  public void setAddress(String addr);
  public void setAddress(Datagram reference);
  public void setData(byte[] buffer, int offset, int len);
  public void setLength(int len);
}
```

Interface javax.microedition.io.DatagramConnection

```
public interface DatagramConnection
    implements Connection {
  // Methods
  public int getMaximumLength();
  public int getNominalLength();
  public Datagram newDatagram(int size);
  public Datagram newDatagram(int size, String addr);
```

```
  public Datagram newDatagram(byte[] buf, int size);
  public Datagram newDatagram(byte[] buf, int size, String addr);
  public void receive(Datagram dgram);
  public void send(Datagram dgram);
}
```

Interface javax.microedition.io.HttpConnection

```
public interface HttpConnection
    implements ContentConnection {
  // Constants
  public static final String GET;
  public static final String HEAD;
  public static final int HTTP_ACCEPTED;
  public static final int HTTP_BAD_GATEWAY;
  public static final int HTTP_BAD_METHOD;
  public static final int HTTP_BAD_REQUEST;
  public static final int HTTP_CLIENT_TIMEOUT;
  public static final int HTTP_CONFLICT;
  public static final int HTTP_CREATED;
  public static final int HTTP_ENTITY_TOO_LARGE;
  public static final int HTTP_EXPECT_FAILED;
  public static final int HTTP_FORBIDDEN;
  public static final int HTTP_GATEWAY_TIMEOUT;
  public static final int HTTP_GONE;
  public static final int HTTP_INTERNAL_ERROR;
  public static final int HTTP_LENGTH_REQUIRED;
  public static final int HTTP_MOVED_PERM;
  public static final int HTTP_MOVED_TEMP;
  public static final int HTTP_MULT_CHOICE;
  public static final int HTTP_NOT_ACCEPTABLE;
  public static final int HTTP_NOT_AUTHORITATIVE;
  public static final int HTTP_NOT_FOUND;
  public static final int HTTP_NOT_IMPLEMENTED;
  public static final int HTTP_NOT_MODIFIED;
  public static final int HTTP_NO_CONTENT;
  public static final int HTTP_OK;
  public static final int HTTP_PARTIAL;
  public static final int HTTP_PAYMENT_REQUIRED;
  public static final int HTTP_PRECON_FAILED;
  public static final int HTTP_PROXY_AUTH;
  public static final int HTTP_REQ_TOO_LONG;
  public static final int HTTP_RESET;
```

```
    public static final int HTTP_SEE_OTHER;
    public static final int HTTP_TEMP_REDIRECT;
    public static final int HTTP_UNAUTHORIZED;
    public static final int HTTP_UNAVAILABLE;
    public static final int HTTP_UNSUPPORTED_RANGE;
    public static final int HTTP_UNSUPPORTED_TYPE;
    public static final int HTTP_USE_PROXY;
    public static final int HTTP_VERSION;
    public static final String POST;

    // Methods
    public long getDate();
    public long getExpiration();
    public String getFile();
    public String getHeaderField(String name);
    public String getHeaderField(int n);
    public long getHeaderFieldDate(String name, long def);
    public int getHeaderFieldInt(String name, int def);
    public String getHeaderFieldKey(int n);
    public String getHost();
    public long getLastModified();
    public int getPort();
    public String getProtocol();
    public String getQuery();
    public String getRef();
    public String getRequestMethod();
    public String getRequestProperty(String key);
    public int getResponseCode();
    public String getResponseMessage();
    public String getURL();
    public void setRequestMethod(String method);
    public void setRequestProperty(String key, String value);
}
```

Interface javax.microedition.io.InputConnection

```
public interface InputConnection
    implements Connection {
  // Methods
  public DataInputStream openDataInputStream();
  public InputStream openInputStream();
}
```

Interface javax.microedition.io.OutputConnection

```
public interface OutputConnection
    implements Connection {
  // Methods
  public DataOutputStream openDataOutputStream();
  public OutputStream openOutputStream();
}
```

Interface javax.microedition.io.StreamConnection

```
public interface StreamConnection
    implements InputConnection, OutputConnection {
}
```

Interface javax.microedition.io.StreamConnectionNotifier

```
public interface StreamConnectionNotifier
    implements Connection {
  // Methods
  public StreamConnection acceptAndOpen();
}
```

Package javax.microedition.lcdui

Class javax.microedition.lcdui.Alert

```
public class Alert
    extends javax.microedition.lcdui.Screen {
  // Constants
  public static final int FOREVER;

  // Constructors
  public Alert(String title);
  public Alert(String title, String alertText, Image alertImage,
      AlertType alertType);
```

```
   // Methods
   public void addCommand(Command cmd);
   public int getDefaultTimeout();
   public Image getImage();
   public String getString();
   public int getTimeout();
   public AlertType getType();
   public void setCommandListener(CommandListener l);
   public void setImage(Image img);
   public void setString(String str);
   public void setTimeout(int time);
   public void setType(AlertType type);
}
```

Class javax.microedition.lcdui.AlertType

```
public class AlertType {
  // Constants
  public static final AlertType ALARM;
  public static final AlertType CONFIRMATION;
  public static final AlertType ERROR;
  public static final AlertType INFO;
  public static final AlertType WARNING;

  // Constructors
  protected AlertType();

  // Methods
  public boolean playSound(Display display);
}
```

Class javax.microedition.lcdui.Canvas

```
public abstract class Canvas
    extends javax.microedition.lcdui.Displayable {
  // Constants
  public static final int DOWN;
  public static final int FIRE;
  public static final int GAME_A;
  public static final int GAME_B;
  public static final int GAME_C;
```

Package javax.microedition.lcdui

```
    public static final int GAME_D;
    public static final int KEY_NUM0;
    public static final int KEY_NUM1;
    public static final int KEY_NUM2;
    public static final int KEY_NUM3;
    public static final int KEY_NUM4;
    public static final int KEY_NUM5;
    public static final int KEY_NUM6;
    public static final int KEY_NUM7;
    public static final int KEY_NUM8;
    public static final int KEY_NUM9;
    public static final int KEY_POUND;
    public static final int KEY_STAR;
    public static final int LEFT;
    public static final int RIGHT;
    public static final int UP;


    // Constructors
    protected Canvas();


    // Methods
    public int getGameAction(int keyCode);
    public int getHeight();
    public int getKeyCode(int gameAction);
    public String getKeyName(int keyCode);
    public int getWidth();
    public boolean hasPointerEvents();
    public boolean hasPointerMotionEvents();
    public boolean hasRepeatEvents();
    protected void hideNotify();
    public boolean isDoubleBuffered();
    protected void keyPressed(int keyCode);
    protected void keyReleased(int keyCode);
    protected void keyRepeated(int keyCode);
    protected abstract void paint(Graphics g);
    protected void pointerDragged(int x, int y);
    protected void pointerPressed(int x, int y);
    protected void pointerReleased(int x, int y);
    public final void repaint(int x, int y, int width, int height);
    public final void repaint();
    public final void serviceRepaints();
    protected void showNotify();
}
```

Interface javax.microedition.lcdui.Choice

```
public interface Choice {
  // Constants
  public static final int EXCLUSIVE;
  public static final int IMPLICIT;
  public static final int MULTIPLE;

  // Methods
  public int append(String stringElement, Image imageElement);
  public void delete(int elementNum);
  public Image getImage(int elementNum);
  public int getSelectedFlags(boolean[] selectedArray_return);
  public int getSelectedIndex();
  public String getString(int elementNum);
  public void insert(int elementNum, String stringElement,
      Image imageElement);
  public boolean isSelected(int elementNum);
  public void set(int elementNum, String stringElement,
      Image imageElement);
  public void setSelectedFlags(boolean[] selectedArray);
  public void setSelectedIndex(int elementNum, boolean selected);
  public int size();
}
```

Class javax.microedition.lcdui.ChoiceGroup

```
public class ChoiceGroup
    extends javax.microedition.lcdui.Item
    implements Choice {
  // Constructors
  public ChoiceGroup(String label, int choiceType);
  public ChoiceGroup(String label, int choiceType,
      String[] stringElements, Image[] imageElements);

  // Methods
  public int append(String stringElement, Image imageElement);
  public void delete(int index);
  public Image getImage(int i);
  public int getSelectedFlags(boolean[] selectedArray_return);
```

```
  public int getSelectedIndex();
  public String getString(int i);
public void insert(int index, String stringElement,
      Image imageElement);
  public boolean isSelected(int index);
  public void set(int index, String stringElement, Image imageElement);
  public void setSelectedFlags(boolean[] selectedArray);
  public void setSelectedIndex(int index, boolean selected);
  public int size();
}
```

Class javax.microedition.lcdui.Command

```
public class Command {
  // Constants
  public static final int BACK;
  public static final int CANCEL;
  public static final int EXIT;
  public static final int HELP;
  public static final int ITEM;
  public static final int OK;
  public static final int SCREEN;
  public static final int STOP;

  // Constructors
  public Command(String label, int commandType, int priority);

  // Methods
  public int getCommandType();
  public String getLabel();
  public int getPriority();
}
```

Interface javax.microedition.lcdui.CommandListener

```
public interface CommandListener {
  // Methods
  public void commandAction(Command c, Displayable d);
}
```

Class javax.microedition.lcdui.DateField

```
public class DateField
    extends javax.microedition.lcdui.Item {
  // Constants
  public static final int DATE;
  public static final int DATE_TIME;
  public static final int TIME;

  // Constructors
  public DateField(String label, int mode);
  public DateField(String label, int mode, TimeZone timeZone);

  // Methods
  public Date getDate();
  public int getInputMode();
  public void setDate(Date date);
  public void setInputMode(int mode);
  public String toString();
}
```

Class javax.microedition.lcdui.Display

```
public class Display {
  // Static methods
  public static Display getDisplay(MIDlet c);

  // Methods
  public void callSerially(Runnable r);
  public Displayable getCurrent();
  public boolean isColor();
  public int numColors();
  public void setCurrent(Displayable next);
  public void setCurrent(Alert alert, Displayable nextDisplayable);
}
```

Class javax.microedition.lcdui.Displayable

```
public abstract class Displayable {
  // Methods
  public void addCommand(Command cmd);
  public boolean isShown();
  public void removeCommand(Command cmd);
  public void setCommandListener(CommandListener l);
}
```

Class javax.microedition.lcdui.Font

```
public final class Font {
  // Constants
  public static final int FACE_MONOSPACE;
  public static final int FACE_PROPORTIONAL;
  public static final int FACE_SYSTEM;
  public static final int SIZE_LARGE;
  public static final int SIZE_MEDIUM;
  public static final int SIZE_SMALL;
  public static final int STYLE_BOLD;
  public static final int STYLE_ITALIC;
  public static final int STYLE_PLAIN;
  public static final int STYLE_UNDERLINED;

  // Static methods
  public static Font getDefaultFont();
  public static Font getFont(int face, int style, int size);

  // Methods
  public int charWidth(char ch);
  public int charsWidth(char[] ch, int offset, int length);
  public int getBaselinePosition();
  public int getFace();
  public int getHeight();
  public int getSize();
  public int getStyle();
  public boolean isBold();
  public boolean isItalic();
  public boolean isPlain();
  public boolean isUnderlined();
  public int stringWidth(String str);
  public int substringWidth(String str, int offset, int len);
}
```

Class javax.microedition.lcdui.Form

```
public class Form
    extends javax.microedition.lcdui.Screen {
  // Constructors
  public Form(String title);
  public Form(String title, Item[] items);

  // Methods
  public int append(Item item);
  public int append(String str);
  public int append(Image image);
  public void delete(int index);
  public Item get(int index);
  public void insert(int index, Item item);
  public void set(int index, Item item);
  public void setItemStateListener(ItemStateListener iListener);
  public int size();
}
```

Class javax.microedition.lcdui.Gauge

```
public class Gauge
    extends javax.microedition.lcdui.Item {
  // Constructors
  public Gauge(String label, boolean interactive, int maxValue, int initialValue);

  // Methods
  public int getMaxValue();
  public int getValue();
  public boolean isInteractive();
  public void setMaxValue(int maxValue);
  public void setValue(int value);
}
```

Class javax.microedition.lcdui.Graphics

```
public class Graphics {
  // Constants
  public static final int BASELINE;
  public static final int BOTTOM;
  public static final int DOTTED;
```

```
public static final int HCENTER;
public static final int LEFT;
public static final int RIGHT;
public static final int SOLID;
public static final int TOP;
public static final int VCENTER;


// Methods
public void clipRect(int x, int y, int width, int height);
public void drawArc(int x, int y, int width, int height,
    int startAngle, int arcAngle);
public void drawChar(char character, int x, int y, int anchor);
public void drawChars(char[] data, int offset, int length,
    int x, int y, int anchor);
public void drawImage(Image img, int x, int y, int anchor);
public void drawLine(int x1, int y1, int x2, int y2);
public void drawRect(int x, int y, int width, int height);
public void drawRoundRect(int x, int y, int width, int height,
    int arcWidth, int arcHeight);
public void drawString(String str, int x, int y, int anchor);
public void drawSubstring(String str, int offset, int len,
    int x, int y, int anchor);
public void fillArc(int x, int y, int width, int height,
    int startAngle, int arcAngle);
public void fillRect(int x, int y, int width, int height);
public void fillRoundRect(int x, int y, int width, int height,
    int arcWidth, int arcHeight);
public int getBlueComponent();
public int getClipHeight();
public int getClipWidth();
public int getClipX();
public int getClipY();
public int getColor();
public Font getFont();
public int getGrayScale();
public int getGreenComponent();
public int getRedComponent();
public int getStrokeStyle();
public int getTranslateX();
public int getTranslateY();
public void setClip(int x, int y, int width, int height);
public void setColor(int red, int green, int blue);
public void setColor(int RGB);
public void setFont(Font font);
```

```
    public void setGrayScale(int value);
    public void setStrokeStyle(int style);
    public void translate(int x, int y);
}
```

Class javax.microedition.lcdui.Image

```
public class Image {
  // Static methods
  public static Image createImage(int width, int height);
  public static Image createImage(Image image);
  public static Image createImage(String name);
  public static Image createImage(byte[] imagedata, int imageoffset,
      int imagelength);

  // Methods
  public Graphics getGraphics();
  public int getHeight();
  public int getWidth();
  public boolean isMutable();
}
```

Class javax.microedition.lcdui.ImageItem

```
public class ImageItem
    extends javax.microedition.lcdui.Item {
  // Constants
  public static final int LAYOUT_CENTER;
  public static final int LAYOUT_DEFAULT;
  public static final int LAYOUT_LEFT;
  public static final int LAYOUT_NEWLINE_AFTER;
  public static final int LAYOUT_NEWLINE_BEFORE;
  public static final int LAYOUT_RIGHT;

  // Constructors
  public ImageItem(String label, Image img, int layout,
      String altText);
```

```
  // Methods
  public String getAltText();
  public Image getImage();
  public int getLayout();
  public void setAltText(String altText);
  public void setImage(Image img);
  public void setLayout(int layout);
}
```

Class javax.microedition.lcdui.Item

```
public abstract class Item {
  // Methods
  public String getLabel();
  public void setLabel(String label);
}
```

Interface javax.microedition.lcdui.ItemStateListener

```
public interface ItemStateListener {
  // Methods
  public void itemStateChanged(Item item);
}
```

Class javax.microedition.lcdui.List

```
public class List
    extends javax.microedition.lcdui.Screen
    implements Choice {
  // Constants
  public static final Command SELECT_COMMAND;

  // Constructors
  public List(String title, int listType);
  public List(String title, int listType, String[] stringElements,
      Image[] imageElements);
```

```
    // Methods
    public int append(String stringElement, Image imageElement);
    public void delete(int index);
    public Image getImage(int index);
    public int getSelectedFlags(boolean[] selectedArray_return);
    public int getSelectedIndex();
    public String getString(int index);
    public void insert(int index, String stringElement,
        Image imageElement);
    public boolean isSelected(int index);
    public void set(int index, String stringElement, Image imageElement);
    public void setSelectedFlags(boolean[] selectedArray);
    public void setSelectedIndex(int index, boolean selected);
    public int size();
}
```

Class javax.microedition.lcdui.Screen

```
public abstract class Screen
    extends javax.microedition.lcdui.Displayable {
  // Methods
  public Ticker getTicker();
  public String getTitle();
  public void setTicker(Ticker ticker);
  public void setTitle(String s);
}
```

Class javax.microedition.lcdui.StringItem

```
public class StringItem
    extends javax.microedition.lcdui.Item {
  // Constructors
  public StringItem(String label, String text);

  // Methods
  public String getText();
  public void setText(String text);
}
```

Class javax.microedition.lcdui.TextBox

```
public class TextBox
    extends javax.microedition.lcdui.Screen {
  // Constructors
  public TextBox(String title, String text, int maxSize,
      int constraints);

  // Methods
  public void delete(int offset, int length);
  public int getCaretPosition();
  public int getChars(char[] data);
  public int getConstraints();
  public int getMaxSize();
  public String getString();
  public void insert(String src, int position);
  public void insert(char[] data, int offset, int length,
      int position);
  public void setChars(char[] data, int offset, int length);
  public void setConstraints(int constraints);
  public int setMaxSize(int maxSize);
  public void setString(String text);
  public int size();
}
```

Class javax.microedition.lcdui.TextField

```
public class TextField
    extends javax.microedition.lcdui.Item {
  // Constants
  public static final int ANY;
  public static final int CONSTRAINT_MASK;
  public static final int EMAILADDR;
  public static final int NUMERIC;
  public static final int PASSWORD;
  public static final int PHONENUMBER;
  public static final int URL;

  // Constructors
  public TextField(String label, String text, int maxSize,
      int constraints);
```

```
  // Methods
  public void delete(int offset, int length);
  public int getCaretPosition();
  public int getChars(char[] data);
  public int getConstraints();
  public int getMaxSize();
  public String getString();
  public void insert(String src, int position);
  public void insert(char[] data, int offset, int length,
      int position);
  public void setChars(char[] data, int offset, int length);
  public void setConstraints(int constraints);
  public int setMaxSize(int maxSize);
  public void setString(String text);
  public int size();
}
```

Class `javax.microedition.lcdui.Ticker`

```
public class Ticker {
  // Constructors
  public Ticker(String str);

  // Methods
  public String getString();
  public void setString(String str);
}
```

Package **javax.microedition.midlet**

Class `javax.microedition.midlet.MIDlet`

```
public abstract class MIDlet {
  // Constructors
  protected MIDlet();
```

```
  // Methods
  protected abstract void destroyApp(boolean unconditional);
  public final String getAppProperty(String key);
  public final void notifyDestroyed();
  public final void notifyPaused();
  protected abstract void pauseApp();
  public final void resumeRequest();
  protected abstract void startApp();
}
```

Package javax.microedition.rms

Interface javax.microedition.rms.RecordComparator

```
public interface RecordComparator {
  // Constants
  public static final int EQUIVALENT;
  public static final int FOLLOWS;
  public static final int PRECEDES;

  // Methods
  public int compare(byte[] rec1, byte[] rec2);
}
```

Interface javax.microedition.rms.RecordEnumeration

```
public interface RecordEnumeration {
  // Methods
  public void destroy();
  public boolean hasNextElement();
  public boolean hasPreviousElement();
  public boolean isKeptUpdated();
  public void keepUpdated(boolean keepUpdated);
  public byte[] nextRecord();
  public int nextRecordId();
  public int numRecords();
  public byte[] previousRecord();
  public int previousRecordId();
  public void rebuild();
  public void reset();
}
```

Interface javax.microedition.rms.RecordFilter

```
public interface RecordFilter {
  // Methods
  public boolean matches(byte[] candidate);
}
```

Interface javax.microedition.rms.RecordListener

```
public interface RecordListener {
  // Methods
  public void recordAdded(RecordStore recordStore, int recordId);
  public void recordChanged(RecordStore recordStore, int recordId);
  public void recordDeleted(RecordStore recordStore, int recordId);
}
```

Class javax.microedition.rms.RecordStore

```
public class RecordStore {
  // Static methods
  public static void deleteRecordStore(String recordStoreName);
  public static String listRecordStores();
  public static RecordStore openRecordStore(String recordStoreName,
      boolean createIfNecessary);

  // Methods
  public int addRecord(byte[] data, int offset, int numBytes);
  public void addRecordListener(RecordListener listener);
  public void closeRecordStore();
  public void deleteRecord(int recordId);
  public RecordEnumeration enumerateRecords(RecordFilter filter,
      RecordComparator comparator, boolean keepUpdated);
  public long getLastModified();
  public String getName();
  public int getNextRecordID();
  public int getNumRecords();
  public int getRecord(int recordId, byte[] buffer, int offset);
  public byte[] getRecord(int recordId);
  public int getRecordSize(int recordId);
  public int getSize();
  public int getSizeAvailable();
  public int getVersion();
```

```
    public void removeRecordListener(RecordListener listener);
    public void setRecord(int recordId, byte[] newData, int offset,
        int numBytes);
}
```

Index